D1621226

Fifty Shelves of Grey

Fifty Shelves of Grey

A Selection of Great Books Erotically Remastered

Vanessa Parody

Constable • London

Constable & Robinson Ltd
55–56 Russell Square
London WC1B 4HP
www.constablerobinson.com

First published in the UK by Constable,
an imprint of Constable & Robinson Ltd, 2012

A copy of the British Library Cataloguing in
Publication data is available from the British Library

ISBN: 978-1-47210-238-6 (hardback)
ISBN: 978-1-47210-227-0 (ebook)

Printed and bound in the UK

1 3 5 7 9 10 8 6 4 2

'If you go home with somebody, and they don't have books,
don't fuck 'em'
– John Waters

Foreplay

Before the internet there were books, and before there was sex, there were sex scenes.

As a girl, my entire sex education consisted of being told not to sit on a boy's lap without putting a phone book on it first. My shoulders ached with carrying the Yellow Pages around in my handbag just in case.

That all changed after a chance encounter with Jilly Cooper's *Riders* – picked up mistakenly by this pony-mad teen. Talk about rude awakening! Within hours I was going through every book in my parents' bookshelves looking for the dirty bits. Who amongst us has not balanced a copy of Jeffrey Archer's *First Among Equals* on their palm to see if there's a well-used place where it falls open? It is a rite of passage as familiar as staying up all night to watch a French film on Channel Four in the hope that two dreamy-eyed *ingénues* will go skinny-dipping together, or at the very least a fat philosopher with a moustache will bang a bored housewife on the kitchen table while she shouts out, *'Mon Dieu, baise moi!'* (subtitled, coyly: 'My God!')

In these less innocent days, all the vicarious shagging a girl could want is available at the click of a mouse, whether in full-colour live-action for home use, or in text downloaded onto a Kindle for discreet consumption on public transportation during one's morning commute to one's disappointing job in digital marketing. Erotic novels abound. One's every fantasy is catered for in each hue of E. L. James's *Fifty Shades of Grey*.

But what of the sexually voracious reader whose tastes are of a more literary bent? The discerning onanist cannot survive on Anaïs Nin and Lady Chatterley alone. Yet even the most dedicated of bluestocking masturbators cannot be expected to trudge through the entire works of Philip Roth looking for the fleeting moments in which an elderly professor is fellated by an eager, illiterate lesbian.

For you, I humbly offer *Fifty Shelves of Grey* – all your favourite books, from *The Lord of the Rings* to *Winnie-the-Pooh*, artfully condensed and erotically remastered, packaged into one volume, and ergonomically designed to be easily read with one hand.

From literary masterpieces – Jane Eyre turns the tables on Mr Rochester; to modern classics – Philip Marlowe is a dick of a different kind in *The Big Sleep*; via philosophy – get intimately acquainted with your Kant; and self-help – the Fear gets well and truly Felt, and we Do It Anyway; with detours into science fiction – aliens and humans enjoy some *entente très cordiale* during *The War of the Worlds*; and even recipes – Nigella Lawson treats herself to some afternoon delight; this collection has something for every reader and every kink. So whip off your glasses, let your hair down and unleash your inner hot librarian.

Vanessa Parody

Contents

1

Jane Eyre

by

CHARLOTTE BRONTË

There was no possibility of taking a walk that day, not for my Mr Rochester; for oh, how the tables had turned since first we met. Then I was but a common governess, and he my master, though he tells me now he was ever in thrall to me: not to my beauty, for I had always but precious little of that; but to my plain, honest ways, my fierce yet subtle intelligence, and to his certainty that, but for propriety, I should like to take him over my knee and give him a good, sound beating.

Nowadays, when we talk late into the night – Mr Rochester attached to a cunning rack of my own devising, while I oftentimes tighten the screws – my beloved husband tells me of the madness in his first marriage to Bertha. For many a year he kept her incarcerated in his attic for his own dark pleasures – or so thought he; but these never did fulfil him. He fancied himself quite the dominant man; never dreaming that he would be more at ease under the direction of a determined, if slightly short, woman. Thus did he continue for years, abusing poor Bertha to their mutual dissatisfaction, until he met me and thrilled to my inner steel. How well he understood me!

Then, of course, came the terrible fire; and though my beloved was initially distressed by his blinding and the loss of the use of his arm & leg, he has now fully embraced the infinite kindness of the Lord's gift in placing him so entirely in my power.

So there was to be no walk, no matter how intense the beauty of the dappled vernal sunshine through the sycamores, nor how alluring the call of the swallows in flight. Instead, I bound my love prone on the conjugal bed – no need for a blindfold, of course; and I prepared my equipment with most thorough care. Mr Rochester has a weakness for my governess days, and so I deployed my cane most assiduously, for the good of his education, and savouring his every cry of delighted pain. Then even those dear sounds grew tiresome to me; so I stopped his screams with one of my stockings in his soft, wet mouth, and fetched the item which we have both come to love the most – a cudgel of sorts, but slim, and assiduously polished. This I greased with lard from the kitchens, and introduced it to the most sacred of places upon my husband.

Reader, I buggered him.

2

Nineteen Eighty-Four
by
GEORGE ORWELL

It was a bright cold day in April, and the clocks reminded
Winston Smith of tits. Ever since he'd been working at the
Ministry of Sex – Minifuck, in Newspeak – everything
reminded Winston of tits. Minifuck was in charge of enforcing
family values, and on the walls of the towering concrete
building – which, to be fair, didn't remind Winston of tits, but
of a huge, hard cock – were the three slogans of the Ministry:

OBEDIENCE IS ORGASM

CHASTITY IS CHOICE

FIDELITY IS FUN

As well as the omnipresent reminder:

BIG BROTHER IS WATCHING YOU. And a symbol of
binoculars.

Winston sat at his desk in a pair of tight, pink EverySlacks, going through the newspapers with a thick black marker pen, looking for indecent images to obliterate. As he could never know what Big Brother would consider indecent, he had developed the perverse ability to see the erotic potential in almost anything, from atomic missiles to parrots. Winston went through more black marker pens than any other employee, and he feared being taken to task for his wastefulness almost as much as for indecency, but so far he had never been reprimanded, and indeed had three times been singled out and brought to the front of the Two Minute Wank for a round of applause, which was all the Two Minute Wank consisted of. They can't see inside my head, thought Winston, as he blocked out a photograph of some shrimp cocktail. Until they can see inside my head I'm safe. But as far as he knew, the Thought Police didn't have a Vice Squad . . . yet.

Just then his supervisor, O'Brien, came over and leaned across the table. Winston inhaled his musk and felt an involuntary twitch in his cock. It's O'Brien, for crying out loud, he told himself. His neck is wider than his head. And yet, something in O'Brien's aura of brutal but intelligent authority couldn't help but excite him.

'Big Brother's been watching you and your enormous black highlighter,' said O'Brien. 'You're going to have to come with me.'

Winston stifled a moan.

He followed O'Brien's taut, grinding buttocks out of Minifuck, into the icy air beyond. The two men did not speak, but when O'Brien led him into that most feared of all buildings, the Ministry of Love, Winston started to tremble, and not in a good way. How did they know his dark, depraved thoughts? Who had betrayed him? Was it that cafeteria worker who had such a sensual way of spinning his tortilla? Or was it just that only someone with an imagination as perverse as his could censor so many innocuous photographs?

Their footsteps echoed down the corridors of Miniluv. Winston counted the numbers on the rooms as they passed. 99 . . . 100 . . . 101. O'Brien stopped.

'Not Room 101!' Winston wept.

O'Brien looked around in surprise. 'Who said anything about Room 101?'

Instead, O'Brien unlocked the door to Room 102.

'What's in Room 102?' said Winston.

'Everyone knows what's in Room 102,' said O'Brien, pushing the door open.

The room was dimly lit, with a lava lamp and a 'Love is . . .' poster. Winston heard the low hum of a saxophone, the seedy wah-wah of 'Take Five' on the tape recorder.

'Remember, Big Brother is watching you,' O'Brien told Winston, and he reached over and pulled him inside by his hardening crotch. 'Big Brother likes to watch.'

The Lord of the Rings
by
J. R. R. TOLKEIN

Frodo shook Sam awake and they set off to find Gandalf, for today was the day of the Great Council of Elronhubbard in which Frodo would finally meet the gathered Company of the Ring and reveal his Ring to them. They found Gandalf waiting in a shady glade beside a bubbling brook, tapping his foot impatiently.

'There you are, young hobbits. Come, the Company are eager to see your Ring.'

He led them to a clearing and there, seated on carved stone seats, were the elves, including a weird-looking one whose name was Legoland from Northern Merkinwood. There were also the dwarves, Groin and Gimlit, a man of Gondor and, of course, Elronhubbard himself, the lore-master.

'Welcome, hobbits. This man is Boromir, I have bidden him join us for he has many questions about your Ring, plus, as you can see, he has a magnificent silver-tipped horn,' said Elronhubbard.

Frodo glanced down towards Boromir's lap and saw that

indeed his silver-tipped great horn was peeking out from his fur-lined cloak and lay upon his knees. He thought to himself, It is true, he has a great horn, but then I am in possession of a Great Ring. We shall make fine partners in the coming struggle. His thoughts were interrupted by Groin.

'Frodo, you are in grave danger. Lord Sauron has heard tell of your Ring and he longs to possess it for himself. He sent word to us dwarves on Lonely Mountain that it is but a little Ring, the least of Rings, but still he desires it.'

'Hey, hey, hey,' said Frodo. 'It is not "the least of Rings", it is a Great Ring. It is tight, if that is what Sauron is getting at.'

'Let us not quarrel,' said Elronhubbard. 'There is no question that your Ring is the Ring to rule all others. We are all bearers of powerful Rings but yours is the One Ring.'

'Thank you,' said Frodo. 'I'm lucky to have good genes – I inherited my Ring from my uncle, Dildo Baggins. But I have taken great trouble to get it here intact so I would appreciate a little respect,' he added, glowering at Groin.

Boromir came and knelt before him, the head of his great horn brushing the grassy floor.

'Frodo, no one disrepects your Ring. We are all here to honour and protect it from those who would wish to do awful things with it. I for one come to warn you of an old enemy of your uncle's who still desires a Baggins' ring for his own. You may remember him as Smeagol, but he likes to be called "Gollum" when he is naked, and he is naked most of the time. Fear not, I have imprisoned him.'

'Meanwhile, the question is what shall we do with this Ring?' said Elronhubbard.

Groin grumbled, 'I would like to see it first and be assured it is the Ruling Ring.'

Frodo was shaken by a sudden shame and felt a great reluctance to reveal the Ring. But Gandalf nodded encouragingly and he took off his mithrel coat and stood naked before the company. He turned and bent to touch his toes. The company gasped. A golden glow came from the Ring. Elronhubbard approached and gently parted Frodo's cheeks.

'It has an inscription. Just as Isildur wrote in his account!'

'Yeah it's in ancient Elvish – it means "Follow your dreams",' said Frodo.

'Er, no. It's in my dialect,' said Legoland, peering into Frodo's deep-cloven way. He read aloud the inscription. *'Ash nazg durbatuluk, ash nazg gimbautl, ash nazg thrakatuluk agh burzum-sihi krimpatul . . .* Roughly translated it says, "One Ring to rule them all, One Ring to find them, One Ring to bring them all and in the Darkness bind them."'

'I'll kill that bloody tattoo artist if I ever get back to the Shire,' said Frodo standing up. 'What else did Isildur say about me?'

'He said your Ring was hot when he first took it, but then it seemed to cool and shrink but without losing either its beauty or shape. He also said it was precious to him though he bought it with great pain'

'Ah, that's nice. OK, shall we get on with this – can we all agree mine is the best Ring?'

The Company of the Ring nodded and they set about honouring Frodo's Ring. Gimlit suggested they turn out the lights or wear blindfolds for a more sensuous experience but in the end the lights stayed on and only he put on a blindfold.

Boromir washed the Ring with water from the icy Silverlode spring in which had been steeped athelas leaves. Some were polishing their weapons in preparation: the spear of Gil-Galad, the sword of Elendril. Gimlit talked loudly about 'preparing to rim the Black Gate of Mordor', and Groin said he would 'return the ring to Orodruin's fire', as he took a bottle of Tabasco from his tunic and shook a couple of drops onto his finger. Legoland meanwhile kept talking about 'felching', which Frodo could only assume was elvish for 'beautiful'.

4

Fever Pitch
by
NICK HORNBY

I never expected to score. Like my team, I was considered notoriously boring, although I did have a fully completed Soccer Star sticker album from 1968 and two spare Frank McLintocks from the same year, which I hoped might be enough to one day impress a football-minded girl into giving me a quick hand job between halves in the toilet at the Highbury Library, as our stadium was unfairly nicknamed. But I was resigned to going home from the nightclub by myself and manfully grinding one out in the style of the classic Adams, Keown, Dixon, Winterburn back four. No offence to Steve Bould, who was also key in that era.

But I attempted an audacious pass anyway – the sort of speculative pass that Liam Brady would make in his pomp, often seeking the trusty head of the mercurial Irishman Frank Stapleton. And I got a surprise result, though maybe not quite as surprising as the extraordinary ninety-second-minute Michael Thomas goal which, against all odds, won us the Championship at Anfield in 1989, ending eighteen years of hurt, which was almost as long as my sex life had been dormant, since Kathleen Potts let me put my hand up her skirt after football practice one February afternoon in the Lower Sixth. Preferring to play the first leg with home advantage, I took her back to my place.

She lifted her top like the legendary Charlie George lifting both the First Division trophy and the FA Cup in the historic 1971 Double-winning season, a feat only previously achieved by Spurs in the twentieth century, and took down her knickers like Sammy Nelson dropping his shorts after his late equalizer against a gritty Coventry side in 1979, an incident for which he was fined – rightly in my opinion – two week's wages by club bosses. I appreciated her strip, and she proceeded to handle my balls in a way that happily reminded me of the late Sir Bert Millichip making the FA Cup third round draw.

Not wanting to get caught offside, I took it slow at first, starting off by kissing her breast, my lips pressed against it like Pelé's on the Jules Rimet trophy, won an unprecedented three times by the South American genius. I don't know why the smooth Brazilian came to my mind at that point. She moaned her encouragement, so I grabbed hold of her Clock End with both hands and pulled her to me. It felt so Ian Wright, Wright, Wright. I hadn't been this excited since Andy Linighan, of all people, scored the goal that won George Graham's Red and White Army the Double in 1993, albeit in a replay, and it was the slightly less prestigious Cup Double this time. I didn't try to explain the difference to her; women just don't get it. And anyway, her Cup Double was really something. Andy Linighan played most of that match with a broken nose courtesy of a nasty elbowing from Mark Bright. Remarkable. What a hero.

At half-time I stopped for fifteen minutes and ate an orange.

Then we did some quick stretches and started again, this time facing in the opposite direction. Before I could unleash my sliding tackle I wondered if I could get away with taking a dive in her box. The trouble was, I'm just not that sort of player. In my opinion, diving is the curse of the modern game. Ray Kennedy never dived, and he managed a not unimpressive 71 goals in 212 games for the Gunners.

Just as I was wondering if I was going to be pulled off, I finally spotted an opening. It was tight, but it was there. Like Brian Talbot I've always been adept at playing in the hole, so I went for it. Unfortunately, in my excitement I shot far too soon. She saw it coming from a mile off, and I made a terrible mess. I was reminded that you should never attempt to lob Seaman from distance.

I had to accept that she had been badly fouled. I rightly received my marching orders, though, ironically, she was the one who needed an early bath. I hadn't been so disappointed since Graham Rix missed the spot-kick which saw us lose the 1980 European Cup Winners' Cup Final to Valencia via the lottery of a penalty shoot-out.

But it wasn't a dead loss, because she let me take her up the Arsenal the following Saturday. Home game against Everton – we won 3–2.

5

Feel the Fear and Do It Anyway
by
SUSAN JEFFERS

Michael has a fear of flying. Sarah has a fear of death. Daniel has a fear of being asked to sing 'O Mio Babbino Caro' at stag weekends and missing the A flat. What I tell them all is that they are NORMAL. In fact they are more than NORMAL they are MORENORMAL.

But the GREAT thing is that FEAR LEADS TO GROWTH, though it is also fair to say that in some cases, growth leads to fear. Particularly if you ride the subway through north Queens any time after 11.30 p.m. opposite a man in loose pants. The point is not to fear the fear but FEEL THE FEAR. Give the guy a hand. Literally. Do it. I do. It's powerful and spontaneous. Everyone wins.

THOUGHT:

We have to get into a position where we enjoy the idea of MULTIPLE OUTCOMES. In multiple positions. With all kinds of people in all kinds of scenarios.

Donald has an overbearing boss at work, a bully he despises. Now imagine if Donald were to go into the office one day, look his boss in the eye, strip naked and say, 'I am breaking through old patterns and moving forward with my life', and then languidly stroke his hardened member across his boss's freshly bought half-fat blueberry bagel. What's the worst that can happen? NOTHING AS BAD AS DONALD'S ALREADY IMAGINED!

In Donald's case his bravery and 24/7 commitment to Self-Help led him to adventures outside of the office and eventually to being arrested for masturbating on a protected wind farm. But you know what? Donald fears nothing now. Not even the pending environmental lawsuit. And that, dear friends, is POWER.

6

The Big Sleep
by
RAYMOND CHANDLER

She was a cool drink of water, two bazooms, a couple of the longest pins you ever saw, two peepers and a schnozzle. Sure, she had the full set all right. And anybody could see she was a tough little number, you could tell by the sneer on her lovely mouth and the jujus she was smoking out of both nostrils. I tried to get up, but the crafty broad had put me in bracelets while I was jingle-brained and I didn't want to give anybody the impression I didn't know how to accessorize.

'What's the big idea, sister? You want to tell me why you've got me trussed up like a Christmas turkey?'

She took a step towards me, turned the roast potatoes pinning down my ankles, and then levelled a thirty-eight straight at my jewels.

'Supposing I answer you by blowing that little brooch of yours clean off?'

'Wait,' I said. 'It was my mother's and the setting is antique.'

'Give me one good reason.'

'You don't get it, sugar. I'm not some two bit gangster, I'm a dick.'

'You're telling me.'

'I mean I'm a detective, baby. I can tell you what happened to Gums McGee. Remember him? The wise guy you took for a sweetheart 'til he made off with your virtue and your xylophone?'

'Keep talking,' she murmured. The gun was still fixed at my chest but her hand was shaking.

'A little bird told me he's back in town, maybe I can help you find him.'

'Oh yeah? That little bird's been a whole lot of chatty and I don't set no store by it anyways. Especially since he turned up croked.'

Her eyes flicked to the sideboard and I followed her gaze. My blood ran cold. The little bird was a stiff and no mistake – its beak was blue and its feathers matted.

'You blipped off the bird? OK, I get it, you're a big shot, I'll squeal.'

'You bet you will, brother,' she said and, to my surprise, untied me. 'Now take off your pants. If you're such a big dick, I want to eye your privates.'

I didn't know what this broad was playing at, but I liked her style and I stripped. Watching me the whole time, she drank me in, like an elderly Bulgarian man enjoying a bowl of soup after a salty goulash. Before I had time to bounce the last sock off my elbow, she launched at me like a Texan at an oil spill for a roll in the hay that would have straightened the Tower of Pisa.

I was just lighting up a Lucky when the door burst open and

a dwarf in a raincoat snapped a picture of me naked as the day I was born and just as surprised.

'Say cheese,' said the dame, as she buttoned up her dress. I felt like a boob. It was all a flimflam. I'd bought myself a whole lot of Dutch and I sure as hell wasn't the kind of cat who liked waffles.

7

Mrs Dalloway
by
VIRGINIA WOOLF

And so she found herself that morning at St James's in a delightfully ostentatious drawing room belonging to Colonel Pickenfoot, who being a robust bear of a man and boasting the boorish, rosy cheeks of a predator startled unduly from enjoying a half-masticated owl, had also, curiously, the eyes of a shifty pig trying to sell her life insurance for a deceased uncle.

And yet. And yet . . . Perhaps it was the intoxicating scent of the fresh-cut lilies on the windowsill that overwhelmed her at that moment with their whisper of velvet-draped opium dens and silken-skinned courtesans and caused her to throw aside her lavender blue dress with the fine French lace that a kindly Breton crone had once sold her on a disappointing day trip to Rennes; and run free, a slightly mottled Thetis, past the Colonel with his snort of surprise and through the French windows; windows she had not thought to open at first, thus causing her to bounce off them a few times before bursting forth; and hence forging a path through the damp dew-swept grass (upon which she had once enjoyed an awkward June picnic with the

Colonel's plump, clammy-handed son, newly down from Oxford) and upon which she now knelt down and rolled. She had the sense, as the Colonel and his visitors, Mr and Mrs Popcote of Littlewane, watched her through the shattered window frame, with her fingers quite splayed upon her most secret bud, that they were perhaps casting judgement and yet she cared not. Oh, the ecstasy! (She was forcibly removed an hour later by the local constabulary and spent a rather desultory night in a cell, unfurnished.)

8

Three Men in a Boat
by
JEROME K. JEROME

Boffing is suggested – on Montmorency and boffing – George's skin – dear old nanny – steak and porter – temperance ladies – the perils of backing up

'So, chaps,' I said, 'have you ever boffed on a boat?'

There were four of us – George, and William Samuel Harris, and myself, and Montmorency, although Montmorency was a dog, so my remark was not primarily addressed to him. As we know, dogs boff everywhere. Harris said he had not boffed on a boat, and George claimed half a point, because he'd given himself a hand shandy in a dugout canoe once.

'And chaps,' I said, 'have you ever boffed another chap?'

(Again, Montmorency was not included in the question. Dogs boff everything. I often think it would be awfully jolly to be a dog, boffing along, and never having to do any work of any kind.)

'Not since school,' said George.

'Come on, George,' said Harris, 'everyone knows *Tom*

20

Brown's School Days doesn't count. I've only boffed girls,' he added, 'or, to be honest, thought about boffing girls, except for an encounter with one lady of the night, who it might be more accurate to describe as a matron.'

'Well,' said I, 'here's a jape to be had. Here are three chaps, and here is a boat. Why don't we all boff on this boat?'

The chaps agreed that this was a capital idea, though George was worried he might get sunburned, exposing unaccustomed skin to the open air. But he proved more agreeable to the notion when we decreed that he go on the bottom, and so be shielded from the sun.

'A chap has sensitive skin, you know,' he said. 'He cannot help it but he does.'

So George put a pair of pillows under his knees to protect himself from splinters and got down on all fours, and Harris put what he insisted on calling his bratwurst in what he insisted on calling George's hot cross bun, and I did to Harris what a chap does when he loves another chap very much, or so my dear old nanny used to tell me, and off we boffed.

All went well to begin with. Who doesn't like boffing? Though George complained a bit that he was getting crushed under our weight – we had overindulged a hair on the steak and porter – and I was sore that Harris was getting twice as much fun as the two of us, and Harris was just sore, and Montmorency wouldn't stop barking, because he didn't like boffing to be had if he weren't the one having it, and we weren't about to let a dog join in; a chap has standards.

But then the boat rounded a corner in the Thames. To this day I don't know how the boat rounded the corner. Must be the tides, or whatnot. All I can say is that when George or Harris is involved in navigation we invariably hit the bank. But with us three chaps involved in a boff sandwich, the boat did a lovely arc all by itself, and then drew level with a group of picnicking ladies from the Temperance Society.

'Back up! Back up!' shouted George.

Harris quite misunderstood George's intention and pulled himself right out, exposing that engorged German sausage of his to the now-shrieking ladies, killing off any chance we might have had of claiming to those good women that we were simply practising Greco-Roman wrestling in the healthy open air, and giving me a right old thump in what he insisted on calling my Spanish onions at the same time, causing me to bark even louder than Montmorency.

'Well dash it all,' said Harris, 'that was a terrible idea of yours.'

9

The Art of Love
by
OVID

Just as José Mourinho's expert coaching took Chelsea to the top of the Premiership, so under my tutelage you will soon be able to find and seduce even the most resistant of modern women. With my careful counsel she will quickly become the meek Clegg to your Cameron, the whimpering Becks to your Posh, the hint of vanilla in your overpowering Shiraz.

How to Find Her
At Work: The office has long been a favoured hunting ground, but you will have to continue your employ in the same building and there is a good chance that she will tell everyone how small your cock is. And possibly disribute photocopies.

At the Gym: The gym is no place for artifice and will give you a more accurate idea of what you're getting. Her pulsing neck veins as she lifts 120 kg on the bench press will give you a good sense of how your target may look in the throes of passion, but this is unfortunately also true of your high-pitched whimpers as you wrestle with the thighmaster.

In the Sauna: On the upside you get a professional unlikely to be shocked by your requests, but you lose all the fun of the chase and repeat visits get expensive, especially for anything really perverse.

How to Win Her

It is customary for women to pretend they're not interested when in fact they're imagining doing the hokey-cokey on your wonky donkey even as they claim they've got book group on Thursday. Be confident and follow these simple steps, and you will secure your prey with bonds stronger than any leather restraint.

Get Her Friends on Board: Or at least neutralize them, but not by sleeping with them. Firstly you risk spreading your efforts thin, and secondly you risk spreading chlamydia.

Buy Her Stuff: Presents work. An early underwear gift will set the tone and direction. It's only a short step from tasteful lace to crotchless panties and nipple tassels, and from there you are well on the way to clamps, ball gags and reins.

Good Personal Hygiene: Men frequently fall at this hurdle, but if you want any part of you licked at any point it is in your interest to make sure that you showered in recent memory, your pants are not crusty and your toenails won't send her running for the hills.

And so my friends, my work here is done, set the wreath of myrtle upon my perfumed hair. As Tony Blair did, and Bill Clinton before him, I will set up a foundation and earn out my days on the after-dinner speaking circuit. I have given you the weapons you need to vanquish the tricksiest of females, but whoever overcomes an Amazon with my sword, at his moment of climax, let him shout with gusto: 'Ovid was my master!'

Winnie-the-Pooh
by
A. A. MILNE

In which Winnie-the-Pooh gets into a rather difficult position with Rabbit.

Pooh always liked a Little Something at eleven o'clock in the morning, and he was very glad to know that Rabbit did too. He was surprised, however, that this morning Rabbit hadn't laid the table with the usual plates and mugs, but rather he had left it completely bare, except for a few lengths of rope and a bright red silk handkerchief. 'Now listen, Pooh,' said Rabbit, his ears erect and quivering with excitement, 'I've had an idea. It's quite an Unusual Sort Of Idea but I think you'll like it very much. For you and I are going to play a game.' Pooh's fur went quite pink and bristly with joy and he did a merry little dance.

'Oh good,' said he, 'for I do love games of all kinds.'

'I rather thought you might,' replied Rabbit, a touch sinisterly, thought Pooh. And then he ordered the bear to climb up on to the table and remove his shirt.

The table was very cold on Pooh's back and he wondered if

he should say something, but Rabbit was so busy tying his arms and feet to the table legs he decided he probably ought not to bother him. So he busied himself making up a song about tables instead. Before long, Rabbit appeared by Pooh's head again, this time holding a large pot of golden honey. 'Is that for me?' cried Pooh. 'I do hope so, for I'm most awfully hung–' But poor Pooh found he couldn't finish his sentence because Rabbit had stuffed the red silk handkerchief right into his mouth where it felt all scrunchety and rough.

'Ah, that's better!' exclaimed Rabbit. 'For a bear of little brain you do talk an awful lot. Besides, I'd rather just look at you, as he traced his paw along the inside of Pooh's furry thigh.'

To Pooh's surprise Rabbit then did something very strange. Using a large spoon, he carefully dripped some honey right on to his belly, where it slowly dribbled downwards in a long gloopy strand. Then, fixing Pooh with a look that made Pooh's very toes twitch with fear, Rabbit said sternly, 'I know how much you want this honey, Pooh. But I'm going to have it. All of it. For I'm going to lick every last teeny tiny drop up until you're sparkling clean.' Pooh's eyes widened; what on earth could this mean? As Rabbit's ear-tips swept over his belly, Pooh suddenly thought he should have heeded Christopher Robin's advice and worn some trousers. Suddenly he felt like a Very Naughty Bear Indeed.

Fight Club
by
CHUCK PALAHNIUK

The first rule about fuck club is that you don't talk about fuck club.

The second rule about fuck club is that you don't talk about fuck club.

Maybe at lunch the waiter comes over to your table and he can barely walk because you spent three hours last night between his thighs, riding and riding, first this way up then that way, forwards, backwards, whatever, till he's screaming and he can't breathe and eventually all sweat and saliva he gasps out stop, stop, you're killing me, but you don't say anything except I'll have a chicken Caesar salad, dressing on the side, hold the croutons, because you don't talk about fuck club, and also you only have a twenty minute lunch break and if you started talking about fuck club then you might forget to mention about holding the croutons, and you're off gluten.

You saw the boy who works in the copy centre, a month ago all you had to say to this boy is that the paper feeder is jammed and the photocopier needs more toner and does he have one of those little things you use for pulling staples out, you can't remember what it's called, the de-stapler thingy, Christ, why don't they give those things a name, but now you worship this boy as a deity because you saw him go hardcore on a senior vice president in charge of account liaisons with a severe obesity problem and back hair, and pound him until he went limp and had to stop. That's the third rule of fuck club. If anyone goes limp, the fuck is over.

The fourth rule of fuck club is that you don't wear aftershave or scented lotions, because Tyler has allergies.

The fifth to seventh rules of fuck club are mostly dress code.

The first fuck club was just me and Tyler pounding each other. We were in Bed, Bath and Beyond, where I was shopping for ceramic tiles, and Tyler said I want you to fuck me as hard as you can.

I said to Tyler, I'm not gay.

Tyler said, It's not gay to fuck a man. It's gay to fuck women.

OK then, I said, but let's put down some towels first.

By the end of the fuck, we were surrounded by a ring of store employees, clapping and cheering us on, until management got wind of it and broke it up, and now we're banned from all domestic interiors stores on the Eastern seaboard, except Home Valu, because they are grateful for the extra custom.

We're not supposed to talk about fuck club but nobody said anything about posting clips online and now every week there are more and more men and I don't know what to do about it. I need to have a chat to Tyler about how to make these men go away but I'm not sure how to raise it. Tyler can be a little touchy.

Meanwhile every time I go to a damn conference I recognize

all the sales reps and middle managers and non-executive partners just from the uncomfortable way they are sitting and the terrible stubble rash, and we acknowledge each other by quietly handing over a tube of antiseptic ointment.

Later my boss will ask me how I know so many of these guys.

Book club, I say.

The first rule about book club is that you don't talk about book club.

12

The Portrait of a Lady
by
HENRY JAMES

Isabel replayed the morning's events in her mind. She wasn't sure but she thought that maybe she and Pansy had rubbed bustles outside the Duomo. Perhaps it was an overenthusiastic response to the Eucharist, but she just couldn't fathom it. She cursed her American naiveté. What she needed was some sound advice from someone urbane, someone who understood these peculiar European customs. She wasn't sure she was brave enough to go to Madame Merle with her dilemma – but who else had the sophistication to apply to this awkward situation?

She found the lady in the drawing room. The beauty of the Beethoven sonata she was playing took her breath away. Was there no end to Madame Merle's accomplishments? Apparently there was not, for she was playing the piano with her feet whilst dissecting a bee with one hand and rolling a cannoli with the other. One could tell Madame Merle had lived on the Continent for some time.

'Dear me, I hadn't heard your arrival, or I would have

changed into something more elegant.' Madame Merle crawled out suavely from underneath the piano and smoothed the seventeen layers of silk evening gown she was wearing. Isabel immediately regretted her outfit, it felt so American. She nervously adjusted her Stars and Stripes top hat.

Feeling too fraught to address the subject about which she'd sought the lady out, Isabel instead crossed to the window to admire the likeness Madame Merle had recently styled of Benjamin Disraeli in a privet hedge. It was as she was contemplating its magnificence that she suddenly felt a hand snake around her from behind, cupping a breast. She couldn't quite put her finger on it but there was something unusual about Madame Merle.

'Tell me, do you like ladies?' murmured Madame Merle, a feverish excitement in her small grey eyes. Isabel thought of Pansy, of her dear friend, Henrietta, of her kindly Aunt Touchett. 'I do,' she replied.

'I thought so. You've come to the right place, my dear. Florence is bursting with lesbians.'

'Excuse me?'

'But my dear, it is very continental indeed to throw off the chains of servitude to men in favour of cunnilingus with a bosom friend with bosoms.'

'It is?'

'Why yes. We also enjoy bicycling, striding around the countryside in comfortable shoes and a laissez-faire attitude to bathing, although that last trait is merely European. We are all Sapphists here you know. Lady Pensil is a huge aficionado of the strap-on, hence the nickname, Miss Climber likes to tip the velvet hanging from the chandelier and the Countess Gemini likes it up both passages with any object you can find, the dirty puzzle. What's your proclivity?'

Isabel was ashamed. How very American of her not to have a proclivity. She panicked: 'I enjoy tennis.'

'Oh for heaven's sake, I thought you were all about independence. Live a little, why don't you?'

And in an instant Madame Merle had vanished beneath her tea dress, going at her like a raccoon up a chimney stack. Isabel gasped. How perfectly divine this was. Madame Merle was accomplished indeed, she seemed to be everywhere at once, or maybe that was just static. In any case it was magnificent. She shuddered with pleasure: Isabel Archer was clearly no lady. She'd have to cancel getting that portrait done.

13

The Road Less Travelled
by
M. SCOTT PECK

Life is difficult. It is full of difficult decisions. Sometimes you will have to choose between two roads. One is the road more travelled. And one is the road less travelled. You may think the choice is obvious. You may think that you should choose the road more travelled, because that is the road that everyone else has chosen, and so it is probably the better one. But I am here to tell you that you are wrong. You should choose the road less travelled. The road less travelled is the more fulfilling of the two roads. That is why this book is called *The Road Less Travelled*. Although once enough people have chosen the road less travelled it will become the road more travelled, and then I will write a book called *The Road More Travelled*.

The thought of the road less travelled may not appeal to you. It is darker. It is narrower. It smells worse. It is a less comfortable journey all round. It may strike you as a road that should be walked down, but never up. You may have become fond of the road more travelled, that easily-accessed, well-lubricated road. But life is not meant to be easy. It is in struggle that we find our greatest satisfaction. So turn your back on the road more travelled, literally. And take a different path. Do not worry. I will help you. So will Vaseline, if you have any handy.

You may say, I do not think the road less travelled is for me. I am very happy with the road I already have, thank you. I'm not even sure how to get onto the road less travelled. The entrance seems a bit small. There is only one way, and that is through discipline. Discipline is the means of spiritual evolution. If you can't achieve discipline by yourself, ask for help. It is amazing how motivating a man with a firm hand can be, when negotiating the road less travelled.

There are four aspects to discipline that you must master to fully appreciate the blessings of the road less travelled.

1. Delaying gratification. Delaying gratification is the process by which we learn to meet and experience pain first, and then enjoy pleasure. Your journey along the road less travelled may not feel good immediately. In fact you may find yourself thinking, What on earth am I doing on this road? I don't like this road at all. This is a terrible road. But if you persist, if you push on through the pain, through the psychological walls you have built up around yourself and through the occasional moments of unexpected, excruciating embarrassment, you will wonder why you ever used to take that boring old road more travelled to Yawnsville.

2. Acceptance of responsibility. You have made this decision to travel this demanding route. Nobody has made you. So it is no good complaining about it when

you're halfway down and it isn't exactly what you expected. Turning back after you've committed to the journey is very unfair on your travel companion.

3. Dedication to the truth. Never be afraid to say: I am afraid. I have cramp. I need more lube.

4. Balance. If necessary, prop yourself up with pillows.

Don't be disheartened if your voyage is long, hard and uncertain. Extraordinary flexibility is a must for success on the road less travelled. Learn to adapt. Only then will true satisfaction, fulfilment and pleasure be yours.

14

The Fall of the House of Usher
by
EDGAR ALLAN POE

As the evening shade drew on, I finally came within view of the melancholy House of Usher. At first glimpse I was at once gripped with a sense of such insufferable gloom, a depression of the soul so deep, that I regurgitated some cheese. Which was odd as I'd had chicken for lunch. Inside the mansion it was even worse. There was an atmosphere so peculiar, foetid and pestilent, as if a hundred corpses had burst out of their graves and then gone for a long cross country run without bothering to bathe afterwards. Yet I was tired and I also recalled that my old school friend, Roderick Usher, had a sister, Madeline, who was both handsome, affectionate and, due to myopia and a lazy eye, not particularly choosy if one approached her from the left.

Upon my entrance into the equally stinky drawing room, my old friend arose from the sofa on which he had been eating a pungent curry, and greeted me with such overdone warmth that I was forced to take a step back to avoid a cumin-tinged kiss on the mouth. His spirits quickly faded however, as he proceeded to tell me how the morale of his existence had been quite destroyed by the constant fear and revulsion he felt towards the house. Personally I felt this was nothing that could not be remedied by opening a window and throwing out a few bathmats, but he would not be consoled. As night rolled in against the smeared, latticed windows, my feeling of unease grew, until all at once the heavy oak door banged open and before us stood Madeline, wild eyed and pale of pallor. To my astonishment she passed slowly by us, blew her nose loudly on the curtains and then floated out again. 'My sister has been trapped in an otherworldly stupor for days,' lamented Roderick, 'she is possessed by Evil.' 'Yes, I see,' I replied, humouring him. Though clearly she just needed to wear her glasses.

Later, I was enduring a night of fretful sleep due to an intense horror of the hand towel situation in the guest bathroom, when I sensed a figure at the foot of my bed. Before I could scream, it had lifted my bedclothes and night chemise and was working a hungry tongue up and down the insides of my lower calves. Every nerve in my body tingled as the stranger licked and suckled their way upwards until I was engulfed entirely in sensation. Thrashing in ecstasy I cried out, 'Madeline! You have undone me!'

'I'm not Madeline,' replied a male voice. 'Dear God, what phantom was this?' 'It's Roderick. Sorry, I may have misread some signals.' At this moment, the moon shone brightly and morbidly through the clouds, illuminating the shamefaced visage of Roderick, my old friend and unwelcome lover.

Leaping from my bed and stubbing my toe macabrely on the nightstand, I screamed, 'Where is Madeline?' But Roderick just stood, fixing me with a depraved grin so wicked and devilish that it caused my insides to pop out through my shirt briefly.

38

Finally he replied, 'I have interred Madeline in the family vault, or third guestroom, for her soul has withered and died.' 'She hasn't died', I said, 'she just needs new lenses,' but Roderick threw his head back and merely cackled.

I ran from the House of Usher, which was clearly about to fall, for when I slammed the front door, the turret dropped off.

15

The Da Vinci Code
by
DAN BROWN

Robert Langdon ran his fingers through the greying hair at his temples, a sign of maturity, which made him look grizzled in a distinguished way, not unlike a young Harrison Ford or slightly older Tom Hanks, depending on who was available. He, who held a Professorship of Symbolologism from the world-famous Harvard University, in Cambridge, Massachusetts, near Boston! Surely the solution to this puzzle was not beyond his abilities! He had to find it! Where was it?

The young brunette in his bed at the Paris Ritz in Paris turned over in her sleep. She was a numerary assistant of the secretive Catholic organization Opus Dei, and, until he had grazed his mouth over her mortifications of the flesh exactly ten hours and seventeen minutes previously, a celibate. She was also the most beautiful religious extremist he had ever seen. Which made his current predicament all the more excruciating.

Of course a man of his prodigious learning could not have got where he was today, which was sitting up in bed in the biggest, most elaborate suite at the Paris Ritz in Paris, next to a sleeping nun, the night before a very important lecture at the Louvre, France's equivalent of the Smithsonian and home of the famously enigmatic painting the *Mona Lisa* by Leonardo da Vinci, without having heard of the mythical G spot, the seat of a woman's sexual pleasure and, legend had it, almost as good as a penis on the orgasm front. But nobody had ever found it. The Catholic Church, in their hateful quest against everything that brings pleasure and joy, had made sure of that, hiding all evidence of its existence and denying that it was even a thing.

Except that a cadre of devotees of the original, real Jesus, who was a proper man who had sex with Mary Magdalene and enjoyed it, had, with remarkable foresight and striking irony, hidden the location of the G-spot in an intricate religious code, slipped into the Bible, painted into frescoes, carved into the very fabric of the cathedrals where the sex-hating Catholics said their evening matins.

He'd spent years working on the code. Followed the pointing fingers of saints and the manual stimulation they implied. Deconstructed the looks of sexual satisfaction on the faces of serene Madonnas. Even the very word God was part of the code – for what is it, if not a G and then a spot? (He hadn't yet figured out the significance of the d.) And all these years of investigation had led him to here, this very bed, this very woman.

And so the night before, he'd held her in his arms, decoding her breasts, tasting the erudition of her lips, discovering the secrets hidden in her buttocks, until he'd reached the very pinnacle of his life's work, and he finally had the courage to say to her, 'Where is it? Where is the G-spot?'

'Don't you know?' she'd said.

41

'No! Of course not.'

'Well then, you're not much of a man are you?'

With that she'd rolled over and started snoring, leaving him in torment. Typical Catholic.

16

The Old Curiosity Shop
by
CHARLES DICKENS

Assembled in the parlour of Mrs Quilp were some half-dozen ladies of the borough of Tower Hamlets, partaking of high tea and idle gossip. Mrs Quilp herself was a gentle, pretty little thing, but there could be discerned in her blue eyes no small anxiety. She was pining for her husband, the hunchbacked, boss-eyed, polio-ridden, hairy-backed, smelly dwarf Mr Quilp. For though he treated her unkindly she had bound herself to him by those vows that no man may tear asunder, and yet Mr Quilp was out every night a-gambling and a-whoring leaving his wife to yearn for his attentions however meanly meted out.

Just as her mother was ladling more shrimps onto her generously buttered toast, there was a timid knock at the door. Mrs Quilp daintily ran to answer, hoping it may indeed be her Lord and Master returned early to beat her about a bit, because he did care after all. She bit her lip in disappointment to see the angelic figure of little Nell huddled in the porch clasping a velvet bag to her side.

'Mrs Quilp, I've come from the Old Curiosity Shop, hoping to catch your lady-friends. May I come in?'

Mrs Quilp ushered Nelly's slight figure into her bower and introduced her to the ladies gathered there.

'This is Little Nell. Her grandfather owns the Old Curiosity Shop.'

'I have brought a special few old and curious things here for your perusal,' said Nell, drawing from her bag strangely shaped parcels of tissue paper, and setting them one by one on the table. 'Ladies, we are the weaker sex and our husbands care not for our intimate requirements.'

So saying, Nell unwrapped the parcel closest to her, revealing a figure in jade. It was in form a sort of undulating slowworm emerging from a carved lotus-flower.

'Curious indeed,' ventured one of the company. 'What is't, Nell?'

'It is an artificial penis,' answered the sweet slip of a thing.

There was a chorus of coughing and Mrs Quilp's mother – who was stout because she was unsympathetic – demanded brusquely, 'Is this appropriate? Jist how old are ye, child?'

'I'm four and twenty. I look younger because I've been on the baccy since I was eight and it's stunted me. Just like my friends Tiny Tim and Artful. Tim is a year older than I, and Artful is fifty-eight.'

Since she had a captive audience, Nell continued unwrapping her wares, chattering all the while.

'Oh yes, I am quite, quite poor now, but one day with these little tea parties I shall be ever so rich – and then I shall open a franchise chain. All selling delights such as this Chinese dildo from the fifteenth century.' She invited one of the ladies to run her finger over the surface, which was textured with little bumps.

'These ribs and notches will heighten your pleasure.' As she proceeded to unwrap more antique relics, the ladies fell upon them overcome by curiosity. Only Mrs Quilp hung back timidly. Seeing this, Nell took up a parcel and addressed her directly, 'Mrs Quilp, I should like to demonstrate this last rarity for you. Shall we step into your sleeping-closet?' And with that, Nell left the room and Mrs Quilp followed dutifully.

The two women settled on the bed and Nell drew the curtains shut. From the tissue paper she extracted a string of pretty marble balls.

'Is it a necklace?' asked Mrs Quilp.

But Nell answered her not. Instead she reached up through Mrs Quilp's underskirts and touched her there with the cool of the marble balls. Mrs Quilp felt an involuntary rush of pleasure and let escape a tiny sigh. Nell leaned forward and kissed her neck, her décolletage and then her lips, all the while allowing her little hands to explore the softness between Mrs Quilp's legs.

'Tush, tush,' said Nell, her hair hanging loose and her face flushed. 'Now see if you do not prefer these curious Geisha beads to Mr Quilp's poor attentions!' She took up the silken string of balls and began gently to push them into Mrs Quilp. As she did so, pretty chimes rang out. Mrs Quilp moaned softly. Nell pulled on the beads a little, then with her petite fingers pushed them back in, teasing Mrs Quilp into a frenzy. When she could contain herself no longer, Mrs Quilp's bright eyes dimmed with tears and she cried out, 'You are an angel! Such a sweet, tender-hearted angel!'

Nell felt Mrs Quilp collapsing around her teeny-tiny fingers and she withdrew her hand, leant her head upon Mrs Quilp's soft bosom and fell asleep there.

Emerging later from the boudoir, they found all the ladies vanished, and all the curios gone.

17

Blink: The Power of Thinking Without Thinking

by

MALCOLM GLADWELL

Studies have shown time and again that when it comes to making decisions in fast-moving, high-stakes situations, it's frequently the case that the less we know, the better the decision we make. That's really what my message is – don't get bogged down in reams of data and research, trust in the snap judgement of your unconscious.

Let's take, for instance, the case of Ana. She has decided that she's ready to lose her virginity, a key moment in the life of a young woman. She's offered a choice of two contenders to assist her: Jose, a university friend whom she has known for years, and Christian, a multi-millionaire business man whom she has only met a couple of times. Jose is around the same age as her, has obviously been sexually drawn to her for a long time, and is totally trustworthy. He is also incredibly boring. Christian is significantly older, weirdly distant with her and on their second date he tried to get her to sign a contract committing to sadomasochistic sex. He too is incredibly boring but in a different way.

If Ana had been thinking consciously, weighing up the options and evaluating the pros and cons as received wisdom recommends, Jose would be the obvious choice. The sex would be hygienic and safe, he'd cook her breakfast the next day, be nice to her parents, read the map when they got lost in the car, notice when she saw a necklace she liked and then surprise her with it, take her to the airport and collect her after trips, watch subtitled films with her, let her have all the orange and purple Skittles, not leave shaving stubble in the sink, do his share of the laundry, buy her favourite flowers for no reason and not because he's having an affair, and floss.

But Ana allowed herself to be led by her instinct. The smell of leather emanating from Christian's Red Room of Pain was an immediate and overwhelming aphrodisiac and, thanks to her split-second decision, Ana now regularly has upwards of four earth-shattering orgasms a day. Could Jose have provided that? Of course not.

18

The No. 1 Ladies' Detective Agency
by
ALEXANDER McCALL SMITH

One evening, when Mma Ramotswe was watching the sunset with her husband, Mr J. L. B. Matekoni, proprietor and head mechanic of Tlokweng Road Speedy Motors, a young man burst into the room in a state of some distress.

'Mma, I need your help,' he said.

'What is it, Rra?' said Mma Ramotswe.

'My girlfriend wishes to have sex with me and I do not know if I can comply. I am a man of no sexual experience at all. In short, I am a virgin.'

'Do not worry,' said Mma Ramotswe. 'That is what the No. 1 Ladies' Escort Agency is for. Mr J. L. B. Matekoni, please give this young man a cup of Roibos tea, and then we will begin.'

Mr J. L. B. Matekoni put the kettle on and removed the cup featuring the picture of Sir Seretse Khama, President and father of Botswana, from its special shelf, while Mma Ramotswe went into the back room to disrobe. As a modern lady, but of traditional build, she was the perfect person to guide a young man through his first intimate encounters. Her breasts and buttocks were welcoming, unthreatening and huge, three important factors described in her professional bible, Clovis Anderson's *Principles of Enlightened Sex Work*, and she was willing to participate in all activities that did not violate the laws of her country or of good taste and decency. She put on her soft pink dressing gown and went back into the main room.

'Would you feel more comfortable having intercourse with me straight away, or would you prefer to watch Mr J. L. B. Matekoni and myself first, in order to learn the basics?'

'Thank you, Mma. I think I will watch.'

'Very well, Rra. Let us commence.'

Mr J. L. B. Matekoni washed the engine oil from his hands and undid the fly of his navy-blue overalls. 'I will now put a condom on,' said Mr J. L. B. Matekoni. 'Your girlfriend will appreciate your consideration in this matter very much,' said Mma Ramotswe as Mr J. L. B. Matekoni penetrated her and started moving his hips back and forth.

Mma Ramotswe made the sounds which indicated pleasure. At times like this she tried not to think about Note Mokoti, her first husband, a jazz trumpeter and very bad man who was a lion in the sack. Mr J. L. B. Matekoni lacked Note Mokoti's skill with a woman, not to mention his breath control, which had come in very useful in the bedroom as well as the nightclub, but he was a kind man and an excellent role model for the young people of Botswana. This did not stop Mma Ramotswe having the occasional clandestine encounter with the two young apprentice mechanics who worked with her husband at Tlokweng Road Speedy Motors, but this was largely for research purposes.

'Thank you, Mma Ramotswe,' said the young man, putting down his teacup. 'I think I am ready to try now.'

Mr J. L. B. Matekoni detached himself and the young man removed his trousers and climbed on.

'You have a very nice vagina,' he said.

'Thank you, Rra,' said Mma Ramotswe. 'It is very important to pay compliments. Your girlfriend is a lucky young woman.'

This praise caused the young man to ejaculate immediately.

Not for the first time, Mma Ramotswe felt the satisfaction of a job well done.

'Mr J. L. B. Matekoni, would you put the kettle on now?' she said.

19

The Three Musketeers
by
ALEXANDRE DUMAS

The Shoulder of Athos, The Six-Pack of Porthos and the Balls of Aramis

'Zounds, that was some workout,' exclaimed Aramis as the three musketeers hit the showers of M. de Treville's gym in the rue du Vieux Colombier.

'*Morbleu*, gentlemen, thanks for spotting me in that last engagement!' cried Porthos, dropping his doublet to the floor of the changing room, revealing his tight six-pack glistening with sweat.

'*Sangdieu*, I need a good massage for this shoulder,' shrieked Athos, working his fingers over the rippling muscles of his left shoulder. In three bounds, Porthos was at his side and began to knead Athos's shoulder with his strong hands. As Athos leaned back into him, Porthos kissed his neck softly. Whereupon, Aramis, not to be outdone in the proffering of favours, leapt to his feet and joined them, all at once kissing Athos in the French style and rubbing the pommel of Porthos's sword.

'Why don't we adjourn to the showers, good sirs?' murmured Porthos.

'That's a good idea, because I feel so dirty right now,' breathed Aramis.

'Bags be Piggy in the Middle,' screamed Athos.

So saying, the faithful companions hastened to derobe. They whipped back the shower curtain of an impractical burgundy velvet, and hurtled into the shower. The water cascaded down over their bodies, meanwhile a moonbeam streamed through the high window, silvering their fine and manly lines. Their silhouette was very like to the depiction of athletes on a Greek amphora in the Louvre, and it might be discerned from the outline of their figures that the blood of each was fairly roused. But at this very moment, the heavy drape was swept back once more and standing before the three friends was a handsome young man, tanned with cheekbones high, dusky eyes and a full mouth – the infallible mark of a Gascon. Infallible.

'Aha, good sirs! I see I have interrupted you in your *toilette*,' shouted the stranger.

'No, this is the shower! We're not pigs!' squealed Athos.

'He means toilet as in ablutions, *ma poule*,' sighed Aramis.

'Pray tell, young sir, who may you be? Gascon, certainly – that's obvious. But what is your business?' enquired Porthos.

'I am John D'Artagnan and I seek an audience with M. de Treville about gym membership. And you, gentlemen? It is by no means polite that you should know who I am, and I not know you.'

'We are known as the Three Musketeers,' answered Porthos, undressing the stranger with his eyes.

'Also called the three inseparables. We have pledged ourselves to each other,' added Aramis.

'We come as a threesome,' trilled Athos. 'All for one . . .'

'And one for all!' they cried, chorusing their co-dependent motto.

'Hmmm, a *ménage à trois*. Interesting. "All for one and one for all" – yes, it's not a bad card game, but I've always found "Baccarat" more satisfying or better still "Back Alley", and for those you really need four players.' D'Artagnan smiled as he started to peel off his tabard and woollen doublet. His slender torso was toned, lithe and tanned by the southern sun, the very image of a Greek kouros. The three musketeers gasped as one when he took off his riding hose. For despite his youth, he had what could be deemed a 'greatsword' and it was certain that it would require more than one hand to wield it. D'Artagnan dropped to his knees and, using both hands and his full Gascon mouth (infallible!), he engaged all three at once. He was young, but his handling of their swords betrayed no lack of experience.

'Decidedly the Gascon is a man of spirit!' panted Porthos.

'Take my honour, take my honour,' groaned Aramis softly.

'*Touché*! *Touché*!' yelped Athos.

Jumping to his feet, D'Artagnan made a sudden lunge and thrust with his rapier. Quick-thinking Athos parried with his mouth. The *corps-a-corps* was on the point of reaching its climax when the bloody curtain was again flung open by the delicate hand of a beautiful woman with a fabulous cleavage. At her side stood a gentleman with a haughty demeanour.

'Ah, I thought I may find you all here,' said the lady with a smile, and, turning to her companion, she continued, 'Monsieur de Roquefort-Fromage, allow me to introduce you. These are the famous Three Musketeers: the statuesque Porthos, Fragrant Aramis, and my ex, Athos.'

'What?!' bellowed Porthos and Athos together. ''Ods Boddikins, what the deuce is she talking about? Your ex? What does she mean? O Athos! Your ex! We don't even know you any more! Are you even gay?'

20

One Day
by
DAVID NICHOLLS

FRIDAY, 15 JULY 1988: Emma and Dexter nearly have sex.

SATURDAY, 15 JULY 1989: Emma doesn't have sex. Dexter has sex.

SUNDAY, 15 JULY 1990: Emma doesn't have sex. Dexter has sex.

MONDAY, 15 JULY 1991: Emma doesn't have sex. Dexter has sex.

WEDNESDAY, 15 JULY 1992: Emma doesn't have sex. Dexter has sex.

THURSDAY, 15 JULY 1993: Emma doesn't have sex. Dexter has sex.

FRIDAY, 15 JULY 1994: Emma doesn't have sex. Dexter has sex.

SATURDAY, 15 JULY 1995: Emma has sex! Dexter also has sex.

MONDAY, 15 JULY 1996: Emma doesn't have sex. Dexter has sex.

TUESDAY, 15 JULY 1997: Emma doesn't have sex. Dexter has sex.

WEDNESDAY, 15 JULY 1998: Emma doesn't have sex. Dexter has sex.

THURSDAY, 15 JULY 1999: Emma thinks she might have sex but then doesn't. Dexter has sex.

SATURDAY, 15 JULY 2000: Emma doesn't have sex. Dexter has sex.

SUNDAY, 15 JULY 2001: Emma and Dexter have sex.

MONDAY, 15 JULY 2002: Emma and Dexter have sex.

TUESDAY, 15 JULY 2003: Emma and Dexter have sex.

THURSDAY, 15 JULY 2004: Emma dies. Dexter doesn't have sex as a mark of respect.

21

As I Lay Dying
by
WILLIAM FAULKNER

ADDIE

So this is awkward. Apparently my entire family think I'm dead and they're carting me all over the countryside in a coffin. Yesterday they actually tried to forge a river carrying me. Honestly, they're that stupid. Not one of them can read a map. I did think about letting them know I wasn't actually deceased but was simply sleeping off a night on the mint juleps, but then I thought, why bother? Faking my own death is actually a really good way of getting away from them. Not that I hate all of them. I quite like the middle one, but only because he's the result of some hot action round the back of the altar with the Reverend. That man sure did know how to celebrate the epiphany.

Mmm, yeah, up a bit, up a bit, no down, um, look pretend I'm the body of Christ . . . OK, now we're cooking. Take me, Reverend, take me to the holy land and back again . . .Why, I do believe you've risen again.

But anyhoo, the kids, yes, what a bunch of halfwits. I mean that quite literally. None of them have had the faintest idea I've been sneaking out to the Yoknapatawpha County Swingers Association (single ladies free) most nights. They actually swallowed the lie I told them that I had a cold so they shouldn't disturb me for four days. One of them, can't remember his name, decided this meant I was going to drop dead and actually started building a coffin under my window. I mean, how freaking tactless is that? If I were really dying then, frankly, that would be the biggest downer ever. 'Look outside at the beautiful blue sky that the Lord did bring us this day, Mama.' 'Oh thank you child . . . Oh no wait. I can't see the sky because there's a great big coffin in the way.'

Why, Miss Lawington, I haven't seen you down this way before. Why, thank you, I'm rather partial to this girdle myself . . . but of course you may remove it. Hang on, I may have to suck in. Ow . . . ow . . . ow . . . no the other way . . . yep, OK we're there. And here let me free you from that darned petticoat. My, what a sweet cherry pie . . . oh, Miss Lawington, why what you're doing down there is better than winning first prize at the state fair for my zucchini bread.

But yes, back to my children, here's an example coming up . . .

VARDAMAN
My mother is a fish.

ADDIE
I know. He actually said that, I heard it through the coffin,

which incidentally is a terrible piece of craftsmanship. Five years of school my children had and apparently they're unable to stick six pieces of wood together.

Why, Doctor Peabody, I had no idea you were also a member of our little association. Perhaps you could give me an internal examination of some sort?

And then there's my husband, Anse. There goes a walking pin-up. Not. He's awful. We're talking hunchback, splayed toes (nail-less for Pete's sake) and no actual teeth. Not a one. Plus he believes if he ever sweats he'll die. What kind of a person thinks that? We live in Mississippi for Christ's sakes, you're going to sweat picking up a leaf. You know I wouldn't have married him if it weren't for that crummy teaching job.

Hang on a minute . . . El Stupido's coming back . . . What the hell . . .?

VARDAMAN

'It ain't right. You kilt my maw! She cain't breathe with the lid on her coffin!'

ADDIE

You have got to be kidding me! HE'S GOT A DRILL!

VARDAMAN

'Gonna save you, ma, like a fish. Gonna fix you up wiv' breathin' holes.'

ADDIE

No! Stop it you idiot!

VARDAMAN

'There you go, maw. Boy, I sure do love you.'

ADDIE

Oh that's just fan-freaking-tastic, that is. He's just drilled through my face. I am actually dead now. Oh Hallelujah very much.

22

Cyrano de Bergerac
by
EDMOND ROSTAND

Cyrano has fallen foul of two men who are envious of his wit.

DE GUICHE: This fellow grows tiresome.

VALVERT: Observe! I will proceed to put him in his place. Ahem. You know what they say about men with big noses.

CYRANO: 'You know what they say about men with big noses?' Is that really the best you can do? I can think of twelve dozen ways to speculate on the size of my endowment.

Aggressive: Oi, Big Schnozz. If your nob's as massive as your nose you should chop it off and use it as a draught excluder.

Friendly: What an impressive proboscis! You must be excessive in the cock arena! Nice one!

Descriptive: Gadzooks! You have a whiffer like a longship. Your *baton de berger* must indeed be a collossus of penes, straining mightifully against the heavens like a pink, shiny lighthouse of cock.

Inquisitive: Wow! Did your nose come from your mother's side? Do you have a whopping great penis? Is that from your mother's side?

Kindly: Sorry about the massive snout, old boy. Still bet you've got a big old Mr Winky, eh?

Insolent: Get your adenoidal beak out of my face, you massive dick.

Cautious: Ooh, easy big nose. Don't want to put your back out lugging your third leg about.

Thoughtful: Somebody pitch a marquee, with a nose like that, he's bound to have a willy that'll need shelter from the elements.

Pedantic: I believe that the traditions of British seaside puppet-based entertainment have already invented a man with a nose and a prick such as yours, and christened him Mr Punch.

Familiar: Wotcher cock!

Eloquent: What a volcanic sniffer you possess, dear sir. Your phallus must swing so low as to harvest the ground as you move about.

Dramatic: Is that your nose or a ferret clinging to your face? Watch out for his dong, it'll probably take your eye out!

Enterprising: You know with a snout like that you should really get into modelling. If you're as large down south you could make a killing. My brother-in-law's in the business, let me give you his card.

Respectful: Good heavens, but that's a pleasing set of nostrils. Please allow me to shake you by the balls.

Rustic: Lor luv a duck, ain't you got a whopping sneezer, bet you've got a marrow down your trunks, and no mistake.

Military: At ease, Beaky. I'll bet your cannon fires at a distance.

Lyric: Yay, but your snoot is gargantuan. Your wang must in all truth be Ozymandias, king of kings! Look on its works, ye mighty, and despair!

Simple: Hey, big nose. Yeah, I'm talking to you. Bet you have a fucking gigantic dong.

23

Murder on the Orient Express
by
AGATHA CHRISTIE

Hercule Poirot glanced around the restaurant car at the gathered passengers. The dashing Colonel Arbuthnot was smoking by the window, Victoria Denby was perched by the bar in a scarlet kimono, Princess Dragmeoff was looking furious and ugly as ever in her sable coat at a table to his left, the mysterious Turkish gentlemen spoke quietly to each other in the corner, whilst Celia Wratchett was sobbing into her handkerchief, being comforted by the rest of her bridge four. The Wagon-Lits' conductor, M. Boucle, was the last to arrive. Poirot began:

'*Messieurs et mesdames*, I have called you ensemble to investigate how it is that Mr Wratchett came to find himself attached, completely naked, to the upper berth of his compartment with handcuffs for which there is no key. *Mais oui*! As we know, the unfortunate *monsieur* claims to have slipped and fallen into the handcuffs, which he carries with him for the purposes of *sécurité*, at which point the restraints in question accidentally locked around his wrists, fixing him to the iron supports of the bed. I put it to you, *messieurs et mesdames*, that this is most *improbable*! People do not accidentally fall into handcuffs. Someone attached the handcuffs and therefore someone, on this train, has the key to free him.'

M. Boucle felt his palms moisten. What terrible luck for the renowned Belgian detective to end up on his train! And how had they managed to leave the *malheureux* Wratchett still attached to be discovered by the chambermaid this morning? For a small sum, he was happy to overlook the compartment hopping and bizarre practices of the Stamboul–Calais coach, but he felt sure that the esteemed Compagnie Internationale des Wagon-Lits would not take the same position. He would lose his job and the extraordinary benefits that were his natural due. It was a disaster that must be averted! What could he do to throw Poirot and his cursed little grey cells off the scent?

'I put it to you,' Poirot continued, 'that a number of inappropriate and deviant sexual practices are being indulged in on this train, with the tacit approval of the Wagon-Lits' representative!'

There was a sharp intake of breath around the car. Victoria Denby looked faint and the Colonel blanched visibly. M. Boucle couldn't restrain himself '*Mais non*!' he ejaculated.

'*Arrête*, M. Boucle! Do not pretend it is otherwise. I must ask you to stop this ejaculation and allow me to continue. We have two options. Either I am forced to report these practices to the appropriate *autorité*. M. Boucle you will lose your job, and all of you eminent figures will face public humiliation. Or, you permit me to join with you. It has been many years that I have been longing for a good whipping. I am particularly fond of the, how do you call it, riding crop?'

24

E Void

by

G-ORG-S P-R-C

I'm Mimi (Gallic, innit.) I'm in this disco – music is brilliant – and I clock this hot guy. Hot as in smoking. So I bump and grind my way to his patch. I grin, I pout and I shimmy. I flick my long, shiny hair and it works. This guy grabs my hand and yanks yours truly towards him. I fall into him and my body links with his. For two songs I rub up against him. And naturally, this guy – I'll call him Paul – grows hard. As a third song starts, I kiss his lips, drop my digits to his crotch and play a bit. Paul groans softly. I was throbbing and lustful and up for a fuck. So I took him by the hand to the girls' lavatory. Bust my way in past two girls crying and sharing lipstick. I slam Paul into a bog-slot and jump on him. I whip down his zip and pull out his prick. I'm planning all kinds of licking and sucking, tickling and blowing, prioritizing shaft, but not ignoring balls. Graphic but that's how it was.

But just as I drop my lips to the tip of his phallus, that idiot lifts my chin and says, 'You know what would amplify an orgasm now? You know what would aid this occasion a lot?'

'Um, no, Paul. What?' I ask.

Paul grins. 'What would assist this affair at this instant is an E.'

My libido walks straight out and I follow. I just vanish. I'm possibly a slut, but I'm not a bloody junky.

25

The Metamorphosis
by
FRANZ KAFKA

At first Gregor hadn't considered the cockroach look a particularly sexy one. The idea had been hers, and he'd reluctantly agreed. Anything to liven up the grim monotony of his existence! Every day was the same: the early starts, the gruelling travel, the stresses of selling, his domineering boss. And living with his parents made it so difficult to meet girls. No wonder he'd turned to paying for sex.

But once the outfit was on, he found he liked the shiny hardness of the carapace, how with his many legs, he could reach all of her erogenous zones at once, and how his antennae swept sensuously over her naked body. He was turned on by the smell of the rubber, and the way the tactile surface half stuck, half rubbed against his damp bare skin inside. He didn't give a moment's thought to the fact he couldn't reach the zipper by himself.

By the time she turned him onto his back, he was beside himself with anticipation, desperate for her to wrap herself around his smooth black thorax. But once his insect legs were flailing uselessly in the air, she'd stolen his wallet from the bedside table and climbed out of the bedroom window, and now he couldn't right himself. He was completely stuck. The humiliation! Too awful to bear! How was he going to explain this to his family?

He'd been in this dreadful position for six hours now. He looked over at the alarm clock on the chest of drawers; he was going to be late for work. He'd have to call in sick, but his boss would be suspicious; he hadn't been ill once in all the five years he'd worked for him. He'd be bound to get the medical insurance company involved and how on earth would he explain himself to them? Erotic transformation into an insect was not covered on any of their policies, not even Platinum.

Just when he thought his predicament couldn't get any worse, his mother knocked on the locked door. 'Gregor, Gregor,' she cried. He tried to answer her but found he couldn't speak properly, due to the built-in ball gag in the rubber insect costume. All he could emit was a strange, strangled squeak. Other members of the family, alerted to the fact he was unexpectedly still at home, also came and knocked. When he heard his sister's gentle voice, he literally wanted to die of shame. 'Gregor? Are you all right? Do you need anything? Open up, I beg you!'

Eventually, his father used brute force to break down the door. The entire family gasped with horror to see their beloved son and brother gone, replaced by a monstrous, priapic insect. As his mother fetched the fly swat, Gregor used a final, monumental effort to roll over onto his front, and scuttled away underneath the fridge, never to be seen again.

26

Bridget Jones's Diary
by
HELEN FIELDING

Saturday, 18 March
8st 13, alcohol units 7 (but necessary for lowering inhibitions),
cigarettes 19 (practising smoking seductively), calories 2794
(not including whipped cream licked from nether regions), kinks
explored 4.

Have resolved to become kinky. At lunch yesterday, Jude
mentioned *Grazia* article re: kinks of the stars, and suddenly
whole table in flurry of revelation about exciting non-vanilla
sex lives. Considered mentioning time made Mark Darcy wear
Christmas jumper in bed and say, 'Ho, Ho, Ho', at point of
orgasm but fear this is not what meant. Love of kink clearly
vogueish attitude of liberated singleton, and thus must address
it. Note to self: do not tell Mother. She would insist on
demanding details, imparting vibrator advice etc.

As Mark Darcy and I still not speaking since disagreement
over my behaviour at his chambers Christmas party (entirely
unreasonable on his part as if he had not hung mistletoe, I would

not have kissed boss) called Daniel Cleaver to ask for assistance.

'Looking to get fruity, Jones?' he said. 'As luck would have it I'm off to a sex party tonight, why not tag along?'

Spent rest of afternoon trying on different insouciant sex outfits before settling on same little black dress worn to all occasions. One or two small glasses of Chardonnay to steady nerves. At ring on doorbell almost vomited from unsteadied nerves into handbag containing condoms, hand sanitizer and spare tit tape. Answered door, Cleaver on threshold with two gorgeous gigantaboobed stick insects. Both looked horrified at sight of my gargantuan thighs, but one said politely, 'Hello, Bridget, I am looking forward to fucking you later,' in Russian accent.

'Getting cold feet, Bridge?' said Daniel.

'Absolutely not,' I said. 'Let's go and have kinky party sex.'

At arrival at house, immediately shown into vestibule packed with further bosomy Russians and told to disrobe, thus rendering selection of little black dress total waste of time, and also suggesting should have spent longer selecting under-garments rather than going for all purpose M&S, even if from Autograph range. Russians all resemble Agent Provocateur models who have allowed nothing to pass lips ever except caviar and cock.

Followed friendly Russian into main room filled to brim with barely legal sex goddesses and fully-dressed paunchy middle-aged men in suits. Searched for Cleaver to buy me drinks as nowhere to keep money aside from in bra, which have not done since student days, which practice given up after embarrassing moment when boy got five pound note stuck down throat.

'There you are, Jones!' said Daniel, appearing with pair of Russian identical twins hanging off each arm. 'What's that on your boob? Is it Sellotape?'

Realized with horror that had attached dress to self with tit tape and omitted to remove in vestibule.

'I have a Sellotape kink,' I said.

'I prefer gaffer tape,' said one of the twins, but I was not listening, as across room I caught sight of distinctive shape of antlers, last seen worn by Mark Darcy at Una and Geoffrey's turkey curry buffet. Surely not?

Picked way over writhing heaps of naked bodies to find Mark spread-eagled on torture rack, naked aside from antlers and Father Christmas boxer shorts.

'I never knew you were kinky,' I said.

'It's for a case,' said Mark.

'What's the case?'

'It's in case we get back together.'

I have a boyfriend again! Picked up a whip from floor next to the rack and gave him a good thrashing to celebrate. Note to self: wash hands when get home.

'Bridget?' said Mark when he got his breath back.

'Yes?'

'Is that Sellotape on your boob?'

27

A Socratic Dialogue
(of disputed authenticity)

ALCHESELTSE: Come you only now from the country, Clytoris?

CLYTORIS: No, I arrived some time ago. I have been in the Agora looking for you and wondering that I could not find you.

ALCHESELTSE: It is no wonder you could not find me. I was in the sauna.

CLYTORIS: Ah! I remember meeting Socrates as a boy in the sauna.

ALCHESELTSE: Oh yeah?

CLYTORIS: A noble mind.

ALCHESELTSE: I was accustomed to meet him there myself as a young man. Usually on Tuesdays. But let's just say, I wasn't that focused on his mind . . .

CLYTORIS: Were you in love with him? It is true that the beauty of the mind far outshines that of the body. Though no one can forget his snub nose and stocky frame, his mind lent him the beauty of an Adonis. I am not surprised you fell in love!

ALCHESELTSE: Um, it was more of a sex thing really.

CLYTORIS: On the one hand you may have been distracted by the eager passion of youth, but on the other hand you must have acquired much insight through your conversations.

ALCHESELTSE: He would not shut up while we were doing it. Actually I recall I wrote some of our conversation down in my little black scroll. Let us go together to my house and read.

CLYTORIS: Let us. I am sure you will be persuaded that Socrates was a mighty teacher.

ALCHESELTSE: Here is the roll. I'll get my servant to read it. Olive?

Alcheseltse's servant reads. Clytoris takes an olive.

SOCRATES: Alcheseltse, I see your body is well trained and I am told your mind is just as toned and defined. Tell me, what is knowledge?

ALCHESELTSE: Well, handsome, let's see. The shoemaker knows how to make shoes, the juror has knowledge about being a juror, etc., etc.

SOCRATES: A fine answer. Sit on my lap while we test its mettle. Now, you have pointed to an example of knowledge but you have not explained what knowledge is. What is it that is common to the shoemaker and the juror in their understanding of their trade?

ALCHESELTSE: Why don't you ask me what I know how to do really well?

SOCRATES: Let me be clearer. You have talked of particulars of knowledge, while I asked you about the Form Knowledge.

ALCHESELTSE: So . . . let me see if I've understood you. If you asked me about the Form Penis and I just pointed to your penis, that would be a particular penis. And even if I touched it, it would still just be a particular penis. And even if I took it in my mouth . . .

SOCRATES: All I know is that I know nothing, bla bla, bla, philosopher kings, yadda yadda yadda, I am a midwife assisting you in the labour of birthing ideas. Ah!

Alcheseltse's servant stops reading

CLYTORIS: That is an exceedingly brief account of his dialectic.

ALCHESELTSE: Yeah, well, I used to tune out, but that's the gist of it.

CLYTORIS: You recall nothing more? It is a great pity that you were not able to take fuller notes of his teaching.

ALCHESELTSE: Let's just say we were too busy making pretty interesting shadow puppets on the wall of the steam-room cave . . .

28

War and Peace
by
LEO TOLSTOY

The moment Prince Andrey put his arm around Natasha's slender, supple, quivering waist, and felt her stirring so close to him, the champagne of her beauty went to his head. He felt a thrill of new life and knew he must tell her.

'Natasha, I'm not like other men. There're things you must know about me, dark things.'

What could he possibly be referring to? What could someone as fine and clever and upstanding as Prince Andrey be hiding? Was he a vampire? She longed for Sonya to be at her side so that she too could hear these strange words and together they would be able to properly contemplate them and come to understand their hidden meaning.

'I've lived through terrible things; they've affected me in profound ways that I wouldn't have anticipated, although in retrospect Nurse certainly bears some responsibility. The thing is, Natasha, I feel no fulfilment in the kind of banal copulation that people at this ball participate in. It brings me no sense of being alive, of communing with the other. I need to tie you up with my cravat, I need cries of pain and submission, I need . . . No, I must stop! Your young, innocent ears, I can't defile them any further, such a life is not for you! Probably.'

He felt so wretched. Had he really exposed his secret, most innermost self to her like that? The perverted self that only fifteen carefully selected and legally silenced subs had ever known about? And of course Nurse, who had taught him everything he knew and whose well-worn paddle was still his most treasured possession. Damn Pierre and his Masonic exhortation to the virtue of courage! He was beginning to suspect that Pierre had feelings for Natasha himself and was deliberately sabotaging him.

Natasha looked at him, red as a beetroot, and visibly trying to control her panicky breathing by biting down on her rosebud lips. She'd imagined many things that might be in store for her at her debut ball in those brightly lit halls, surrounded by all the brilliant people of Petersburg, but not this. Sonya and she had spent weeks in joyful anticipation discussing so many scenarios: what they would do and how they would feel. They'd even covered the vampire eventuality. How could they not have talked about this? Inwardly, she cursed Sonya and this most glaring of omissions. How best to respond? What did she feel? Andrey was the most devastatingly handsome man she had ever met, with his cavalry colonel uniform, white stockings and light shoes, and he was creating the most unexpected stirrings in her loins. The quivering that Andrey had felt at her waist was moving south, she felt her breathing quicken and shallow – what could it mean?

Andrey saw Natasha's bright eyes, her heaving chest and heightened colour, he sensed the flaming glow from some inner fire that had previously been doused and he hardly dared hope – could it be that she wasn't going to run away? Could he dare to imagine that one day he might have access to her nubile young body, secure in the knowledge that she had signed the non-disclosure agreement and knew the safe words? He had barely felt more afraid in the fields of Austerlitz as he took her by the hand and said, 'Come with me, my innocent Natasha, and let me give you a debut ball to remember.' As they left the room to the fading strains of the Polonaise, Natasha felt herself to be on the brink of something true and important and was grateful that there was a further thousand pages for her to properly get her head around what it all meant.

29

Dead Cert
by
DICK FRANCIS

He was found at the bottom of the Volga, hoof-cuffed, leather blinkers over his eyes and an orange stuffed in his mouth. It was a dirty end for a three-time Derby winner and it was going to be a hell of a job to keep it out of the papers. I wanted vengeance on the bastards who'd done this and, as I trotted away down an icy Moscow side street, I vowed to get it. I hadn't eaten all day but I realized I wasn't going to be able to get to the turnip in my nosebag until I'd put some distance between myself and Admiral's drowned horse corpse.

It wasn't long before I heard the sound of hooves following me. I began to canter; so did they. I whinnied; so did they. I jumped a small child; so did they. The Kremlin was just ahead. If I could get to Red Square I'd have the chance to break into a gallop. As I rounded the corner and burst out into the open, I felt the wind tear through my mane. I could hear them gasping for air behind me. The ponies!

As I streaked past a man in a fur hat playing a balalaika, I reflected back on my days in Newmarket. Before the hay addiction and the backhanders from Russian oligarchs, Admiral was by far and away the top performer in the stable, and not just on the racecourse. He was a Trojan of a horse, huge and as hard as wood. Eighteen hands high and built like a Chippendale sofa, he was a multiple winner on the steeplechase and in the straw. Race after race I'd gallop behind him, admiring his thundering back view. The sight of his jockey crouched forward over his neck, silk-clad buttocks bobbing up and down over Admiral's sleek hindquarters, stirred a jealous passion in me that I struggled to control. I longed to feel those bunched, tense flanks move beneath mine, to see that neck arch before me in ecstasy. I remembered the day I had returned to the stables early after an unexpected tumble on an easy jump, and disturbed Admiral in a state of arousal. I wanted to make a move then, but he was far out of my league. I had to content myself with those times that the bumps and tremors of the horse box would allow me to jolt up against his firm chestnut rear.

So the facts of his death added up worse than a jockey with a weight in his pocket. Everyone knows horses don't eat oranges, and Admiral never wore blinkers. This was no unfortunate accident. Someone had looked this gift horse in the mouth and it was up to me to find out who.

30

Captain Corelli's Mandolin
by
LOUIS DE BERNIÈRES

How like a woman is a mandolin, how capricious, how fickle. In the golden dusk, when the sun is setting and the cicadas are chirruping, she lies there beckoning me, so seductive, so alluring, and yet when I pick her up and move my fingers over her silken strings, the sound that emerges is horrible: high-pitched and screechy. I say to her: 'My ears, my ears! Antonia, why do you torture me so? Why can't I please you? Am I so inexperienced? Is my fingerwork so poor? I have spent hours practising!' I cast her aside in despair, and stalk out of the room, determined to make her suffer as I do. She treats me like an invading army sent to occupy her by force; it is as though she is hollow inside and made of wood, so unfeeling is her response.

But despite her cruel behaviour I am always drawn back, lured by the sensuous curves of her rounded, pear-shaped bowl-back, her slender, swan-like neck and her oval hole, purfled in pearl and silvers, that orifice of delicious, unbearable promise . . . 'Oh my sweet, sweet Antonia!' I am caught for a second by the pain of the loins' longings then, moistened by my own lust,

I take her up again, more forcefully this time, determined to coax a harmonious moan of pleasure from her resistant fret board, to find my way to her sonorous centre. I strum her until she quivers, I reach across her octaves, finding the elusive chord that sounds a vibrating D of infinite yearning and then I stretch again harder, longer, aiming for a tricky B flat 9, I find it and strike it hard and again and faster and faster and as my dampened fingers move quickly across her strings they slip up to a G sharp of desperate anticipation until, with a shuddering suspended F, we finally come together, man and mandolin.

31

Groundwork for the Metaphysics of Cunnilingus
by
IMMANUEL KANT

Intending to publish hereafter a *Metaphysics of Cunnilingus*, complete with diagrams, I issue in the first instance this Groundwork. This preliminary treatise is nothing more than the establishment of a guide and supreme canon for the pleasuring of woman through the dutiful use of one's tongue.

With regard to the ancients, not a lot of people know that I am a fan of Epicurus. True, I am not big on empirical experience as a way to inform our moral choices, but I must concede that Epicurus was correct in as far as the pleasure or hedone of a woman must be regarded as an end in itself, and good without qualification. Cunnilingus then must be highly esteemed for itself and not as, what is termed in vernacular, 'foreplay'. Hence, it is our moral duty to descend upon our beloved. Thus it may be considered a law.

In order that this action should be morally good, it is not enough that it conform to the law, but it must also be done for the sake of the law. Never regard the pussy as means to an end.

That is, the action is not about bringing her to such heights of pleasure that her inclination should be to draw you inside her. It is to be done for the sake of her pleasure. The former is a selfish hypothetical imperative executed with the end of one's own gratification in mind, the latter a universal duty or Categorical Imperative.

Ergo we should engage our tongues (and I will later postulate, on the extreme boundary of practical philosophy, introduce our fingers) for duty's sake, even though we may not be impelled to it by any inclination – indeed, we may even be repelled by an unconquerable aversion. We aspire to a practical rather than pathological love, seated in the will, and not in the propensities of feeling – in action, not in sympathy. [*Darling, if you are reading this, I'm talking in general terms – you know I love the taste of your Schmetterling!*] Now, as readers of my previous essays will be aware, the Categorical Imperative is that I should never act otherwise than so that my maxim should become a universal law. This means it is fine to think about other women as you are going down upon your own fair one. [*Again, darling, this does not apply to yours devotedly!*]

Now, since a Universal Law must be capable of demonstration, let me say something of practicalities. It is true that not all jewels of the fairer sex are homogeneous in form, and indeed the varied geography of their erogenous zones can be perplexing. What is requisite and necessary is to begin with a subtle dialectic with one's lips and tongue to discern the most sensitive areas. In spite of some of my colleagues' theses, I would urge you not to restrict yourself to the clitoris, but to undertake a free, unboundaried investigation of the whole area, a priori and a posteriori, or as they are termed in common parlance, front bottom and back bottom. We must be willing to experiment with pressure and motion, and, as I say, dare to involve our fingers in this critical examination.

You may recall in a previous tract, I asserted that Autonomy of the Will is the Supreme Principle of Morality while Heteronomy is the source of all Spurious Principles. This holds true for Cunnilingus – do not wait to be asked to go down, but dive straight in of your own free and pure Will.

For those who may be disheartened in their inquiry by their dearest's lack of response, the good news is that moral worth is not derived from the realization of the object of the action, but from the maxim by which it is determined. Only dive. It is the endeavour itself that has moral worth, not its result. Otherwise we stray into the questionable ethics of utilitarianism and orgies. Nevertheless, all arts and handiworks have gained by division of labour and specialization. Therefore if your neighbour is able to work a particular area with greater facility and perfection, invite him to join you, provided your sweetheart be not averse.

Let me conclude by reiterating that, as with other universal laws, judgement is sharpened by experience, in concreto. And that is why at three o'clock every afternoon I vigorously partake of my wife's amuse-bouche – you can set your watch by me! Only through daily practice of duty may we proceed from immaturity to enlightenment. *Sapere audete*!

32

The Alchemist
by
PAULO COELHO

Santiago hesitated at the threshold of the tent of the Alchemist. Now after many years, it seemed the pursuit of his Personal Legend was at an end. His journey had begun in Torremolinos. He had led his flock of sheep down from the mountains of Andalusia to enquire as to the meaning of a recurring dream from a gypsy woman who was conversant in the language of dreams. And she was cheaper than the one in Marbella. He had told her how each time in the dream, a young, hot, Andalusian lovely with Moorish eyes had led him to the top of the Giralda tower in Seville. Each time she had pointed in the direction of the Pyramids of Egypt and when he turned to look, she had whipped her hand inside his simple shepherd trousers and begun to massage his manhood. As her hands explored and insisted, he felt she was massaging not his manhood but his Being. In the dream, as he climaxed, the tower of La Giralda fell away and he spun with the girl into infinite space, spraying his seed across the Oneness. That was when he woke up. The gypsy woman looked a bit nonplussed when he finished. 'Um . . . well . . . it's about hand jobs, isn't it? I mean . . . what it's saying is that you need to cross the desert to seek "the hand". It is the "hand that wrote everything". And it's hanging out around the Pyramids of Egypt somewhere. It's obvious. Ten pesos please, my lovely.'

And so it was he had got an easy ferry across to Tangiers, worked in a glassware shop for a year, then crossed the Sahara, fell in love, joined a caravan and arrived here at the oasis. It had been hard to leave Fatima, a woman of the desert. But even as they had made love in a variety of positions, he knew he would never be satisfied until he had been touched by the ultimate hand of his dream. And he understood that if he did not follow his Personal Legend, his love for Fatima would sour. As he remembered her, naked, warm and wet, his resolve strengthened and he drew back the opening to the Alchemist's tent.

The air inside was sweet with incense. The Alchemist bade Santiago enter and offered him some wine to drink.

'I thought Tradition forbade you wine?'

'If you don't tell, I won't,' answered the Alchemist and Santiago was astounded by his desert wisdom. 'What is it you seek?'

'I am seeking my personal treasure, that is the caress of the hand that wrote everything.'

'Ah. Many have sought a gratification to cancel out their suffering. But that gratification is not to be found in others, only in yourself.'

"What do you mean?" asked Santiago.

The Alchemist made no answer. Instead he took a stick and, stepping outside into the moonlit desert, he drew a dirty picture in the sand.

'Um, what's your point?' asked Santiago.

'Onanism,' answered the Alchemist simply.

'Is that to do with the Oneness?'

'No. They sound similar so many learned men have confused the two. Let's go back inside the tent.'

Once back inside, the Alchemist prepared a little corner for Santiago – he spread some cushions, draped a veil across the space and handed him a small bottle of precious oil.

'What is this?'

'It's the Elixir of Life. A couple of drops of that will make the whole experience much more silky and enjoyable. Now make sure your hands don't have any grains of sand on them – desert hazard. Lie back, relax, explore and enjoy yourself. I will return.'

The Alchemist stepped into the desert to talk to the Wind and the Moon. Santiago lay back. His heart was shy, almost afraid, but he took up the Elixir, sprinkled a few drops on his hand and reached down into the folds of his desert robes. It was as the Alchemist said, he knew himself. He understood what he wanted, he anticipated his own desires and could choose to gratify or withhold to delay and intensify the pleasure. He caressed himself for what seemed like hours. As the point of climax drew near, his body seemed to dissolve and he was simply riding waves of purest pleasure, like the great waves he had seen crashing against the rocks of little old Torremolinos. He saw his whole journey with all its trials and delights pass before him and then, he saw Fatima, once more, naked, warm and wet. As he came, he cried out, "Fatima, I'm coming!'

Santiago collapsed back into the cushions, understanding that he could return to Fatima and be happy with her. For he had the secret of his own hands. If sex became samey, he could return to this place of orgasmic bliss. He had crossed deserts and yet he had held the answer in the palm of his hand all along.

33

The Spy Who Came in from the Cold
by
JOHN LE CARRÉ

East Berlin, January 1963

His hand hovering over the bowl of keys, Leamas could feel the sweat gathering on his brow – he had no idea which set to pick although he was going to avoid the owner of the Volvo at all costs. Smiley had assured him it would be obvious, but it wasn't obvious at all, and now Fiedler was fondling his left buttock and whispering in his ear: 'Come on, Leamas, hurry up. If you pick mine out, he can watch.' Fiedler nodded towards Mundt. 'It's time to choose your keys, Leamas,' barked Mundt. Leamas plunged his hand into the bowl, closed his eyes and thought of Smiley, he was back in the muted anonymity of Cambridge Circus. Smiling to himself.

London, 6 weeks previously

'Let me run it by you one more time,' said Smiley. 'You pretend you're coming home with us, but in fact you're going home with them. Then, when you get home with them, you tell them that you saw one of theirs back at the Circus with us. Go to town on the details, make it as real as you can, cock and balls out, all the fun of the fair. Once the precept of exclusivity has been broken, the gloves are off, or rather the pants are down, and we can really get to work. They'll send you back here to report on their defector, we'll pretend to welcome you back into bed so that you can feed misinformation about our dirty practices to them. Then you'll claim that you miss them and their cute little East German tüsche and plead to be taken back into their fückentrüstencircle. Eventually Fiedler will relent because he finds you irresistible, you'll be eyes down, mouth open, and we can really find out what's going on with Mundt. Got it?'

Back in East Berlin . . .

Clutching the keys to Fiedler's Skoda in his hand, Leamas allowed himself to be led over to the couch, while the rest of the Krauts gathered around. For Queen and country, he thought, For Queen and bleeding country. He closed his eyes. Pray God Fiedler didn't find the deep dark place that Smiley had hidden the bug.

34

How to be a Domestic Goddess
by
NIGELLA LAWSON

Afternoon Delight

This is one of my absolute favourite recipes. Completely dependable, it hits the spot every time, and I find myself coming back to it again and again. It's one I turn to both when I'm feeling stressed and when I just want to celebrate the joy of being alive. My husband is a huge fan too, and occasionally I like to have him around to take over if my arm gets tired, but to be perfectly honest I find the consistency better if I'm left to my own devices.

Start the night before by ensuring that you'll have a bit of quiet in the house. Make plans for everyone to be out, or failing that I tend to banish my husband to the garden and plant the children in front of their favourite DVD. I have even been known to issue bags of crisps in a bid to ensure total non-disturbance. Take a moment to revel in this special time for you. I like to think my recipes are as much about the enjoying the process as the end result, and that is particularly true for this one.

Carefully remove all the wrapping. If I'm in a rush I've been known to leave the outer layers on, but honestly I think this works best when all the skin is exposed to the air. Start at the top, caressing the flesh lightly, sensuously, almost like a tickle. Imagine you're smoothing cream over a particularly delicate piece of confectionery. Cover the whole surface once like this, making sure to get into all the nooks and crannies, this will help to tenderize the meat. On occasions I've used a pastry brush, or even a rubber spatula. Allow to rest for a minute or two, then begin at the top again, but with a firmer hand, kneading slowly but surely as you work your way down, paying particular attention to sensitive zones, much as you'd handle well-risen bread dough. I'd advise avoiding implements and sticking to just your hands this time, it's really about that flesh-on-flesh sensation.

Test with a finger: if it's moist to the touch you're ready for the next step. You can do this with a machine if you like, but I prefer to do it by hand, and have developed a pretty fail-safe technique over the years. Start by rubbing with your fingers, gently at first, like making pastry mixture, but gradually getting faster and faster. I like to picture vigorously beating egg whites into stiff peaks. This is the trickiest part, it's all in the speed and positioning, but if you get it right, the results can be explosive.

35

Moby-Dick
by
HERMAN MELVILLE

'Call me Ishmael,' I said, hoping the stranger with whom I'd shared an amorous night had not already gone through my wallet and discovered I was actually called Steve. As the strapping figure rolled over, I discovered with some horror that the nifty mover I'd seen through an ale-goggle haze as we shimmied across the dance floor, was in fact a heavily tattooed Polynesian harpooner. Good heavens, how much had I consumed? 'Call me Queerqueg,' he simpered, and I was about to ask him with deep apprehension whether he had been tested recently, when I realized with horror that I was in fact face to face with two faces. Although one would be hard-pressed to call the other a face as such, for it was very small. And without any kind of flesh. 'This is Martin. He's an ex, whose embalmed head I'm trying to sell here in Massachusetts.' He winked. 'Would you like to use his eye holes again?' 'Dear God, no,' cried I! 'No problem,' he said. 'How about a cruise? Men only . . .'

I knew the whole thing was a disaster when I caught sight of *The Pequod*. It was the poorest excuse for a party boat I'd ever seen, and I considered asking for my ten dollar 'drinks kitty' deposit back and making a run for it, but what with the 300 lb bulk of Queerqueg loping menacingly about with his ex-boyfriend's skull, I decided I'd just have to bide my time and make my way back to shore later on the inflatable banana boat. Still, I was looking forward to seeing the rest of the party-goers, whom Queerqueg had assured me were a pretty bunch. It was only as we drew anchor I realized with sheer horror that the burly, rough-hewn crew were in fact the only occupants of the boat. Furious, I went in search of the Jacuzzi. Typical of the day I was having, there wasn't one, and to add insult to injury I was hit on by an unattractive Quaker, Starbuck, offering some below par coffee.

As the land melted into the distance, I considered hurling myself into the violent waters and making a swim for it – if I hurried I'd still make Happy Hour – but at that moment a foreboding shiver ran through me. Standing erect on the deck above me was a man of such haunted expression that I wondered if he too was feeling jaded about the lack of spa facilities. Then he spoke. 'My name is Captain Ahab. And I'm searching for the largest Dick in the world – Moby.' At last! Someone ready to party. Though I'd have to clear up that my name wasn't Moby.

36

The Old Man and the Sea
by
ERNEST HEMINGWAY

It was his eighty-fourth day without a catch. The sun had scaled the cotton-streaked sky and reached her zenith. She was a cruel bitch. They called her *jua* in Swahili, meaning 'sun'. He had set out before dawn, heaving the mast on his age-gnarled back down to the skiff and rowing out through the phosphorescent waters of the Gulf of *Mejico* to the great well – a deep of nine thousand fathoms where all kinds of fish gathered in the whirl.

He set the lines of Catalan cordel and settled back into the stern.

'I wish I had a six-pack of *Hatuey*,' he said, knocking back a shot of *aguardiente* instead.

Suddenly, a line stretched taut under his old foot. He felt a trembling pull.

'Don't be shy, fish. Eat well and then I will kill you.'

The tugging grew harder, and then the surface of the water broke. He saw the lavender flash of a tail.

'Marlin. Enormous.'

Just then, the head of a woman looked over the port wale. She was damned nice and pleasant enough.

'Hey, silver fox. Give me a hand. Pull me in.'

He obeyed and went over to haul her in, but hesitated when he saw she was topless.

'It's OK. You can touch. I'd like that.'

She turned in the water so that she was facing away from the skiff. Without a word, he hooked his arms under her armpits to pull her up into the keel. His hands closed under her breasts, which were heavy and full. He felt a stirring in his groin. He landed her and fell back against the tiller, unsure what to do next, since normally at this point he would club his catch over the head and then gut it with a *machete*.

'Thanks, *Viejo*. I do love the touch of an old man. You really know what you are doing. I've been circling you for days, waiting for the boy to leave. Finally, I've got you alone. Take me. Love me.'

She flopped over, brought her face close to his and kissed him. Her lips were pleasantly salty. She explored his mouth softly with her tongue, nibbling and sucking on his lips and moaning softly. He found himself sex-aroused.

'Play with my breasts. Squeeze them. Pinch my nipples. I want to feel your touch.'

But his left hand had cramped (they were sitting at an awkward angle). If the boy had been here he could have helped him.

'Come on left hand, you traitor. Do not fail me now.'

He stretched out his calloused hands and massaged her *tetas*. Her smooth skin and the gentle curve of her belly reminded him of a whore he had known in Pigalle. Paris. She was moaning louder now and pushing her tongue into his ear. She moved his hand down over her belly and he was surprised to find a damp opening just above where the scales of her tail began. It was smooth with no hair and reminded him of some sluts he had drunk caipirinha-sodas with in Rio.

'*Ai, papi*, how I love the rough hands of an honest working man. All the rich-bitch mermen have such smooth, bourgeois fingers.'

He pushed his old fingers inside her and she clung to him, breathing heavily and fumbling with his trousers. She took out his old maleness and began to work it. She excited him greatly and he tried to hold back the semen-rushing by thinking of other things: lions on the coast of Sierra Leone; long, cool sips of hurricanes in New Orleans; his great-aunt Esmeralda.

'I want you inside me.'

She pulled him on top of her. She was as strong as a rhinoceros he had bagged in Malawi. They began to make animalistic, aggressive love, grappling and wrestling in the keel of the boat. It seemed to him it was the original, epic struggle between man and woman, between man and fish and finally between himself and all the women he had loved, the first woman and all those who came after.

He came first, firing his seed deep into her with a clear shot as if his manhood was a W. & C. Scott long-barrel rifle. She in her turn came moaning and shuddering like a bull brought low by the *estocada* of a master torero such as the graceful Joselito in the bullring of Madrid.

'Ah, *Sahib*, you came hard and strong.'

'*Si . . . bueno . . . bof . . .* it's been eighty-four days. My left hand cramps often – it's the one I use on myself. So . . . what say we head back to Havana, hit the *Bodega* and have ourselves a *mojito* or ten?'

37

The Boden Catalogue

Vintage-look linen sundress, £89

We love the ruffled shoulder straps on this gorgeous knee-length swingy dress. Equally perfect for sunny country strolls and for being pushed up around your waist as you are taken vigorously from behind by a farmer, yokel or rural milkman.

Fun polka-dot shirt, £29

The mother-of-pearl buttons on this delicious fifties-look tailored blouse are ideal for ripping open to reveal your tremulous breasts when he can't wait another moment before getting your raspberry ripples in his mouth. Available in three retro shades.

Side-button wide-legged sailor trousers, £59

A firm favourite with you from last year, we've adapted these nautical strides to be even easier to pull down quickly when you need to be good and fucked right now. Features front-facing pockets for a more flattering fit.

Perfect slip-on suede pumps, £129

Johnnie Boden always says that when screwing up against a wall, it's crucial to get the angles right. That's why these sassy shoes come in three different heel heights! Buy one pair for each partner. (We do recommend use of a suede protection spray.)

Question to Model:

—Marceline, what's your favourite sexual position?
—I'm French, so it has to be *soixante-neuf, bien sur*!

38

The Library of Babel
by
JORGE LUIS BORGES

The Library is an infinite, unremitting tessellation of hexagonal galleries. Above and below each gallery is another, *ut apes geometriam*. The Library is a vast and limitless honeycomb. Each gallery replicates its vertical and horizontal neighbour in structure.

The galleries connect to each other by mirrored corridors and spiral staircases. Some men of the Library spend their whole life in one hexagon engaged in the translation and interpretation of texts therein. Some men seek only the monograph of their own existence. As an Inquisitor I roam in search of *The Compendium*, a perfect codex containing the essence of all other volumes. But my task has changed.

Yesterday, in the crepuscular light of the stacks, I was in the Crimson Hexagon lost in perusal of an octavo bound in yellow silk when my auricular faculties were perturbed by an unusual sound. We are only supposed to whisper in the Library. A woman was singing in my environs. I looked up to see a Siren in a diaphanous blouse, her hair caught fast in a bun and glasses balanced on her nose. She leaned over my desk and osculated me forcefully. Then she stood up, walked to end of the shelf and beckoned me to follow. She led me through into the narrow corridor, pushed me up against the mirror and reosculated me.

I was nervous since I was a virgin, as were many men of the Library, but luckily in my peregrination I had encountered a palimpsest written by a Priestess from Samoyedic Lithuania in the fourth century BC that purported to be a manual of sexual congress cataloguing coital techniques with some eye-popping lithographs to elucidate the more recondite positions.

She undid the buttons of her blouse and pulled down the straps of her brassiere. Her obelisks had a pleasing symmetry and constituted a perfect simulacrum of the orbs of Doña Pamela Anderson. I bent to kiss them and thus set about deciphering the syntax, grammar, morphology and clitics of her pleasure. A woman's body is a cryptograph, but I was determined to penetrate her enigmas.

I pulled down her skirt and underneath her sheer panties I could discern the penumbra of her pubic hair. I felt myself swell to Leviathan proportions. I slipped my fingers under the border of her pants and started to explore her garden of forking paths. It was dewy and fresh and I dropped to my knees to taste. She sighed and I pushed my tongue into her arcana.

She interrupted me and pulled me to my feet. She undid my flies and guided my phallus into her labyrinth. I thrust deeper and deeper and the walls pulsed around me. The image of myself penetrating her was reflected ad infinitum in the opposing mirrors and I was dizzied by the thought of penetrating her in infinite dimensions and worlds.

She pushed me away and I was momentarily discombobulated but then she turned towards the mirror. Looking in the glass, she smiled at me infinitely, and then reached back with her hand and once again drew me into her Eleusinian mysteries, this time from behind. Every time I was about to climax she would initiate me in a new juxtaposition of our bodies. Scholars of the flesh, we devised and examined different combinations with the zeal of Cabalists.

Our naked milonga quickened and she came shuddering, uttering the syllables *hlör u fang axaxaxaxaxaxas mlö*, which means 'The moon rose above the river' in Tlönic Ursprache, and in our tongue, 'Oh my God, I'm coming'. My orgasm was contingent and necessary upon the retraction of her vaginal muscles.

We sank exhausted by our endeavours. I succumbed to sopor and contentment with her head nestled on my shoulder. When I awoke, I was alone. She had gone, I know not to which far hexagon. I have abandoned my search for the Compendium and am committed to seek only that Woman. I am no longer an Inquisitor. I am that which they call a Stalker.

39

The Very Hungry Caterpillar
by
ERIC CARLE

In the light of a computer screen a little cock lay totally flaccid on a mouse mat.

He nudged the mouse and – pop! – on to the screen came a tiny and very hungry search engine.

He started to look for some pictures to entertain himself.

On Monday he came across a pair of boobs, but he was still horny.

On Tuesday he came across an amateur home video from the former Yugoslavia, but he was still horny.

On Wednesday he came across a German plumber called Dolf who was helping a *Hausfrau* out with her pipes, but he was still horny.

On Thursday he came across a team of cheerleaders who'd got bored in the locker room and were enjoying a group shampoo, but he was still horny.

On Friday he came across a very fat woman having an unusual dentist's appointment, but he was still horny.

On Saturday he came across a team of Bolivian firemen trying to put out a blaze in a brothel, by forming a naked human pyramid and using only their own bodily fluids, to a soundtrack of Beethoven's 'Ode to Joy' played by a group of lesbian pan-pipers.

That night he was wasn't horny any more.

The next day he erased his browser memory and went for a nice pub lunch with his in-laws.

40

Pride and Prejudice
by
JANE AUSTEN

Within a short walk of Longbourn lived a family with whom the Bennets were especially intimate. Mr Bennet found Lady Lucas far more agreeable than his somewhat silly wife, so was careful to encourage regular intercourse between the houses. As such it was no surprise that after the ball at Netheregions a delegation should arrive from Lucas Lodge to discuss events. The eldest Lucas daughter, Charlotte, a sensible, stern-looking girl of twenty-seven, was Elizabeth Bennet's particular favourite. After the Miss Lucases had been ushered in, and the lengthy but obligatory enquiries about the health of their relatives had been made, Charlotte and Elizabeth escaped to Elizabeth's chamber so that they could converse in private.

'Mr Darcy becomes more intolerable every time I see him,' said Elizabeth. 'He barely speaks, and when he does it is only to insult: "Not handsome enough to tempt me." Indeed! He is such a disagreeable man, I would consider his regard to be a misfortune.'

'My dear Eliza,' riposted Miss Lucas, 'it is a truth universally acknowledged that a single man in posession of an attitude problem must be in want of a good seeing-to. Darcy's interest in you is not in doubt. The real question is whether he is capable of meeting your needs.'

'What can you mean?' said Elizabeth. 'It is well known that Mr Darcy is a man of great fortune with a quite exceptionally well-appointed house.'

'You misunderstand me,' said Charlotte. 'A husband may be useful in so far as he should provide material comforts in the matters of an estate, servants, clothing, vittles, carriages and so on. But you cannot count on a man to bring you fulfilment in all areas.'

Charlotte moved from the window to sit next to Elizabeth on the bed.

'Those of us less in demand due to irregularity of form are obliged to be more pragmatic in our decisions,' she continued. 'I have employed an especially pretty chambermaid who is extremely adept with her hands. My front parlour has never been so well looked after and many a pleasurable afternoon has been spent stoking the fire and plumping the cushions.'

'I already have a chambermaid, Charlotte,' said Elizabeth.

Charlotte sighed. 'It's a metaphor,' she said. 'Lizzy, it was clear to me long ago that I would have to explore alternative solutions when it came to the pleasures of the flesh. Physical love does not only have to be between a man and a woman. After all, who knows a woman's body better than another woman?'

'A man?' said Elizabeth.

'No!' Charlotte struggled to contain her exasperation at her confidante. 'If you will only consent to lying back, I shall demonstrate my meaning.'

With a quizzical expression, Elizabeth reclined on the bed. Charlotte raised her dear friend's skirt and unlaced her pantaloons.

'This,' said Charlotte, 'is called your clitoris. I do not expect that Mrs Bennet has seen her way to educating you as to its purpose. But if you apply a finger, thus . . .' There was a brief pause. 'Or a tongue, thus . . .' A longer pause. Outside, chickens clucked in the yard. 'You will see that I am quite correct when I draw your attention as to its benefits,' concluded Charlotte eventually.

'Indeed,' said Elizabeth, once her breath was entirely restored to her control.

Thus the next time a ball was held at Netheregions, Elizabeth was accompanied by a sweet young lady's maid, newly appointed, and felt quite immune to Mr Darcy's disdain.

41

Zen and the Art of Motorcycle Maintenance
by
ROBERT PIRSIG

Zooming along at well over the speed limit, in order to express our individual approaches to time and traffic regulations, I took in the green countryside as we tore past it. The farmhouses were crisp and fresh, and I enjoyed their openness to life in general through the haze of my exhaust fumes. On the horizon I noticed a cold front approaching from the south-west. Most people wouldn't know what that meant, but given my knowledge of horsepower, road traction and the religious practices of the Cup'ik tribe of Alaska, I knew it was time to pull over at the next rest stop.

I indicated to Matthew and Ann Northwood, my riding companions, that it was time to explore our parallel life paths and we veered into the parking lot of a greasy diner. Ordering some food at the counter, I noticed how Matthew and Ann chose spontaneously from the menu, while I used my wealth of life experience to narrow down the options to a corndog.

Outside, we squatted in the dust by our bikes, eating and

tinkering with valves while the storm drew nearer, symbolizing our mounting indigestion. Perhaps excited by the expertise with which I was adjusting my tappets, Ann suddenly threw down her chicken wing and placed a leathery hand on the backside of my chaps. It was interesting how very in the moment she was as she began to lightly spank me with a tyre lever. Although she was clearly enjoying herself, I felt the application was some-what generalized and I reminded her that with a mainjet as oversized as mine, you've got to have clean plugs because, at high speeds, there's going to be a lot of richness. Ann was going to have to work hard and fast to avoid loping my idle.

Tearing off her leathers, she got down to the job. It was an enthusiastic if workaday effort. I would have done it with more skill, but I was determined to give her the enormous force of heat and explosive pressure inside my engine, so she could feel she'd achieved something that day. It was my gift to her. When you have many gifts, you should share them. But I was abruptly halted in my generosity as I suddenly felt a connecting rod up my crankshaft. Matthew was behind me, pounding me flat. He didn't have a perfectly shaped part compared with my own, but his instrument was adequate.

As they happily worked me over, I pondered the importance of the *a priori* presumption of the continuity of motorcycles and the teachings of Aristotle. Matthew and Ann had no idea I was functioning at such an elevated level, but they were clearly having fun, which is a huge boon to a life as prosaic as theirs. Pretty soon however, utilizing my keen sense of smell and instinctive talent for interpreting the gestures of dung beetles, I detected the approach of a tornado. Efficiently removing my sensor unit from Ann's sparkplug socket, I levered myself off

Matthew who was spinning somewhat out of control in third gear.

Giving them a swift, definitive nod, which is the international motorcycle sign for 'follow me' as well 'yes', 'hello' and 'I have a crowbar up my sleeve, now give me my fucking beer you punk', I leapt onto my bike, mounting it like a virile panther. The engine vibrated to life and I melted into the leather groove of my saddle. Nobody gives me a ride like my 1964 Honda SuperHawk and I was going to take the scenic route to Minnesota. Because Socrates would have.

42

In Search of Lost Time
by
MARCEL PROUST

Many years had elapsed during which nothing of Combray had any existence for me, when one day in winter, on my return home, my mother, seeing that I was cold, offered me some tea, a thing I did not ordinarily take. I declined at first, and then, for no particular reason, changed my mind. She sent for one of those squat, plump little cakes called 'petites madeleines', a perfect scallop-shell of pastry, so richly sensual under its severe, religious folds. And soon, mechanically, dispirited after a dreary day with the prospect of a depressing morrow, I raised to my lips a spoonful of the tea in which I had soaked a morsel of the cake. No sooner had the warm liquid mixed with the crumbs touched my palate than a shudder ran through me and I stopped, intent upon the extraordinary thing that was happening to me.

An exquisite pleasure had invaded my senses, something isolated, detached, with no suggestion of its origin. And at once the vicissitudes of life had become indifferent to me, its disasters innocuous, its brevity illusory – this new sensation having on me the effect which looking at Celeste's breasts often has of filling me with a precious essence. Whence could it have come to me, this all-powerful feeling? I sensed that it was connected with the taste of the tea and the cake, but as I felt the depths of my member palpitate (most inconvenient in front of Mother) I knew that it infinitely transcended those savours.

I cleared an empty space in front of my mind's eye and attempted to recall the distant memory to the surface of my consciousness. Several times over I had to try the task whilst carefully balancing my plate over my lap so as to hide my tumescent penis from Mother. That time with the groundsman in Normandy? But no, it was coffee from his little stove we drank there, with croissants I had bought, and the sensation was completely different. Or with the Marquis de Vaugoubert in Verona? But no, I distinctly remember that we were drunk on dessert wine into which we dipped little Italian biscotti and as a result I hadn't been able to perform to the best of my abilities. Or with Cousin Claudette in Aix? No again, during that hot summer nothing but grenadine had accompanied our *tarte aux fraises* and just the sight of strawberry jam still brings a flush to my cheek.

Then suddenly the memory revealed itself. The taste was that of the little piece of madeleine which on Sunday mornings at Combray (because on those mornings I did not go out before mass), when I went to say good morning to her in her bedroom, my Aunt Léonie used to give me, dipping it first in her own cup of tea or tisane. Ah, Aunt Léonie! How I enjoyed those Sunday mornings and what a pleasant change they were from the incessant self-pleasuring that I indulged during those years and that so worried my parents. I look over at my dear mother now, with this memory newly present in my mind, and recalling her lack of censure when I was late for mass, it occurs to me that she may even have had a quiet word with Aunt Léonie. As I finish my madeleine, berthed by the warm recollection of those Sundays, I am struck once again by the complexity of memory, and how events can seem completely different when viewed backwards through the prism of time.

43

The Pillars of the Earth
by
KEN FOLLETT

A rustling from the woods behind woke Tom. He sat upright and peered into the shadows. At this time of year, with the ground hardened from frost, it was not only men who were starving. Wolves grew bold and ventured south from the highlands of the Pennines. Tom grasped his hammer in readiness. Suddenly, a pungent musk filled his nostrils. If it is a wolf, she be ready for cubbing, he thought. He heard a whistle, 'Phwit phwooo.' It was not the sound of the tawny owl, nor was it any bird call Tom knew, though his father had patiently taught him to identify many in the thickets behind their hamlet. Again it came, 'Phwit phwooo,' and the musky scent became overpowering.

Suddenly, a young woman stepped softly out of the undergrowth. She wore a long, blanched wool cloak and her hair hung loose around her shoulders.

'Phwit phoooo!' she whistled. 'You are hotter than stone-baked bread on a July morning! And what be your name, my honey?'

'Tom. Tom Mason.' They pronounced his name differently in other parts of the country: in Cumbria, he was Tom Stonecutter, in Winchester, where they spoke posh, they said, 'Tom Cathedralbuilder', but here in Ely, with their flat fenland vowels, they called him Tom Mason. 'And what be your name?'

'Ellen. I don't have a patronymic, because I'm a proto-feminist, or witch, really. But if I were to have a name like yours denoting my trade, I guess it would be Ellen Fuckswell.'

With that she dropped her cloak to the leaves. She was naked underneath. She leapt on Tom, pushing him to the ground. She kissed him hard, pushing her tongue into his mouth. She fumbled in his tunic whispering, 'My ex was a jongleur, so I know what I'm doing with balls.' She moved down the transept of his spread-eagled body until her lips hovered over the narthex, more specifically his testicles. She blew on them softly and Tom's already erect column swelled further. She nibbled and tickled then licked up his throbbing pillar and took it into the tunnel-vault of her mouth.

Tom could be passive no longer. He was a master craftsman after all. He examined the bevelled mouldings of her breasts with his rough hands and she sighed in pleasure. Encouraged, he sought her undercroft with his fingers and, finding signs of damp, he pulled her on top of him and eased his chisel into her crypt. She moved her hips gently at first, then building steadily in pressure and speed. Her panted breath grew shallower until she threw back her head and howled. Tom felt her vault climax against his monument. Still inside her, he rolled her over and began to hammer her with his mallet until he came in her niche. Exhausted, they pulled her woollen cloak over them and fell asleep.

The next day he got up and went to work at the Cathedral building-site. He examined the mouldings, checked out the undercroft for wet rot, chiselled out a crypt and then hammered the shit out of a niche with a mallet.

44

Freedom
by
JONATHAN FRANZEN

She was hot and she knew it; sticking out her ample chest and surveying the scene with a coy little cock of the head. Walter increased the magnification on his binoculars. He froze; *she was looking right at him.* He was unable to breathe for a minute as they locked gazes across the thirty-feet cavern between them, although it could have been thirty inches, so intense was the connection. Then she turned and bent over to examine a leaf, showing off an impressively full behind. Walter could tell she was enjoying his eyes on her. For a second, she was bathed in dappled sunlight and her pneumatic little figure was outlined in a halo. Then she jerked upright suddenly, a worm in her beak.

He was surprised by the erotically charged volt that seared through him. It reminded him of a party he'd been to, years ago when he was a student, at a friend's vacation house. After getting wasted on a combination of pot and ageing vermouth, they'd all ended up outside, tearing off jeans and T-shirts and jumping butt-naked into the elegant, kidney-shaped pool. Watching from the sidelines on a sun-lounger as the party descended into an orgy, Walter became increasingly perplexed about the effects of overpopulation on global resources. As the scene before him became more sexually adventurous, boy on girl, girl on girl, boy on boy on girl, he wondered briefly, if the answer was indeed recycling. A pair of golden-skinned, beautiful blonde twins appeared and tried to straddle him, but Walter knew it wouldn't be enough to help save the giant panda. He snuck back inside, temporarily despondent, but was finally able to find release over a poster of an owl.

The bird was hopping towards him now. Walter wanted to take her glossy beak between his teeth and gently bite it. He wanted to run his hands through her feathers, finger the fuzzy tufts of her crown. No – no he didn't. What he really wanted was to take her on a sunset drive through the mountains of southern West Virginia, and then maybe go for pizza and a late movie. Sex was just sex. Sharing your dreams and cheesesticks, that was love. Walter sighed. It was time to go back to the motel.

45

The Prince
by
NICCOLÒ MACHIAVELLI

P.S.

Hi Lorenzo

RE: The Prince in his Bedchamber

Your Magnificence may recall that at the beginning of this little book, I said that all dominions under whose authority men have lived in the past and live now have been and are either republics or principalities. That is not strictly true. There is also a guild of highly trained, very discreet, quite hygienic professionals in Florence who, for a very reasonable fee, will subjugate one to their government and wield excessive authority for as long as Your Magnificence requires. It works out at about forty florins an hour, which is not bad and in the long run is a more economic option than keeping a capricious, wily mistress. And, as I have often noted, the populace are nothing if not fickle, wretched and generally shit. I just think, Your Magnificence, it is easier to go professional sometimes. Throw money at the problem.

The one place a Prince may truly let his guard and hair down is in his bedroom (and may I say how fabulous your hair looks in Sanzio's portrait. I like it short!). A Prince must pass his days acquiring principalities, putting down internal subversion and retaliating against external aggression, all the while avoiding contempt and hatred. Therefore it is most relaxing and restorative to descend from the lofty peak of governance to the lowlands of servitude in the privacy of one's closet.

Now a Prince is not constrained by normal morality, but I would advise Your Magnificence to take precautions to safeguard Your Person. Yes, condoms, but also, although it is delicious to feel the wheal of a well-handled whip, delivered in punishment for one's transgressions, nevertheless as a strategic counter-measure it is well to agree a word in advance that will stay the fury of your sweet Nemesis. I like 'doily', but you can come up with your own. Be playful.

Allow Your Magnificence to submit fully to the rule of your Mistress. Let her vanquish you. As I have said, there is no surer way of keeping possession than by devastation and nothing is more devastatingly sweet than having to sit out a seven-hour cabinet meeting with a butt plug inserted on her orders. She will devise all manner of laws and taxes. And then how sublime it is to tease her wrath with disobedience. She may condemn you with foul language, and chain you like a dog while the tribute she exacts with clamps and suture will provoke such uprisings in your loins!

Should you please her with your subservience she may confer favours upon you and give permission for you to lay siege to her valleys and her highlands. I can assure you, it is so titillating for a man used to taking command to be instead unsure of himself and launch a cautious assault. The consequent aggrandizement of one's Pisa Tower is enough though to urge the invasion and plunder of her Netherlands. But even seemingly broken in battle and utterly conquered, she may yet counter-attack and devastate your arsenal with foreign bodies.

If you remain in any doubt of the refreshing, oxymoronic freedom consequent upon enslavement to a Mistress of the Guild, just remember what Catullus said to the consul Aurelius in the forum back in '56: *pedicabo ego vos et irrumabo* (in the vernacular, Your Magnificence, 'I will sodomize and face-fuck you'). Aurelius loved it.

I posed the question previously whether is better to be loved or feared. I would argue there is nothing more arousing than the commingling of the two.

P.P.S.

Are there any vacancies going in your Court at the moment or soon?

NM

46

The Picture of Dorian Gray
by
OSCAR WILDE

It was as if his soul sank with each ascending stair. As he fumbled with the lock, his hand shook, so that it was a full minute before he was able to turn the key and enter. Dorian cast back twenty years ago to those early days of courtship when he would tear up the staircase, fling open the door, unable to wait one second more to feast his eyes on his one true love: himself. Swaying seductively, Dorian would sashay about the room, undoing a button here, removing a sock there, loosening his satin cravat, shimmying out of his cerise smoking jacket, tossing away his taffeta trousers with a flick of his elegant toes, until he was standing naked and proud in front of his devastatingly handsome self-portrait.

Their lovemaking would take up afternoons, days, weeks. They'd begin by lying next to each other just looking, drinking in each other's beauty, mirror images of unimpeachable perfection. Soon, however, Dorian would be unable to resist himself, kissing and licking the portrait all over, the sour taste of turpentine thrilling his tongue, his inquisitive fingers tracing the outline where the oil had coagulated before it dried, reminding him of his own capricious jism, until he reached such a peak of excitement, he could no longer hold back and would explode into a salty fountain of self-adoration over his own likeness. The sexual magnetism he emanated towards himself was so intense that sometimes he'd have to tear away from a night at the opera, a drink at the club, or a morning of organizing his hair oils just to come to this secret room and fondle the frame.

But now, in the flickering light of the half-burned candle, the room seemed to him to be less like a stage waiting for its star, and more the drear surrounds of a funeral home. Dorian approached the purple velvet curtain that shrouded the corpse of his youth and tore it aside.

Dear God! Would it kill it to make more of an effort? He couldn't have desired himself less. The crows' feet, the double chin, the terrible toupee – what was it made out of, horse? – and, the most recent addition, a pendulous gut. What on earth had his portrait been doing behind that purple curtain? Not enough exercise for one thing.

Perfunctorily tugging off his shoes and breeches, Dorian decided to keep his socks on in hope of a swift exit. Trying to avert his eyes, he imagined himself in the parry and thrust of fencing or the sensual manipulations of clay potting, but it was impossible to overcome his disgust. That revolting face was staring at him in stupid adoration – and, wait a minute, was that hair coming out of its ears? At that moment Dorian Gray realized he was going to have to get out of this relationship once and for all. He cleared his throat and began. 'It's not you, it's me . . .'

47

The Highway Code

This Highway Code applies to England, Scotland and Wales. It is essential reading for everyone: men, women, older people, younger people, persons neither old nor young, persons neither and/or both male and/or female, drivers, motorcyclists and horse riders. Please note that having sex with a horse is illegal on all British highways. Many of the rules in this code are legal requirements, and if you disobey them you may be fined, given points on your licence or disqualified from having sex altogether.

Masturbation
Masturbation is a private activity and should therefore never be undertaken on pavements, zebra crossings, pelican crossings or traffic islands. Masturbation however may be undertaken in designated dogging zones (q.v.) in which case reflective garments should be worn at all times for your own safety. You may masturbate in a parked vehicle provided that the vehicle is your own or you are a designated driver or passenger of the vehicle and the vehicle has not been broken into for these purposes, for example, because you liked the look of the leather

and/or velvet and/or other upholstery. Masturbation is also acceptable in traffic jams (with vehicle moving at aggregate speeds of less than 5 mph) but orgasm must only take place when the car is stationary with the handbrake on. You are reminded that the use of mobile phones for the watching of pornography, calling of sex lines or for any other purpose, masturbatory aid or otherwise, is strictly prohibited at all times.

Sexual Intercourse (Non-Penetrative)

Sexual intercourse (non-penetrative) is defined as any sexual interaction, not involving penetration, which involves two or more individuals, one of whom is the driver. For the purposes of this Highway Code, rules for all in-vehicle sexual intercourse, penetrative or otherwise, that does not involve the driver are categorized under 'Other Distractions Whilst in Charge of a Vehicle'. In an urban or built-up area with traffic lights, with a speed limit of 20 mph to 30 mph, and away from box junctions, manual stimulation is permitted, although only the passenger is permitted to climax while the vehicle is in motion. Extreme caution should be taken close to schools and care homes for the elderly, and when the vehicle is preparing to turn right. Along country roads, single carriageway with speed limits of up to 60 mph, it is advisable to take part in sexual exchanges only if you know the road really well. On dual carriageways and motorways, oral intercourse is permitted with additional stimulus from the left hand only. (The right hand is also allowed in conditions of fog.) The driver must maintain a good view of the road at all times. If an orgasm is oncoming please pull into the left 'slow' lane.

Sexual Intercourse (Penetrative)

Penetrative Sexual Intercourse (vaginal and/or anal) involving the driver is recognized by the Highways Agency as a hazardous activity which must never be undertaken in a moving vehicle. Drivers are encouraged to take advantage of designated dogging areas, as established by the 2010 Byways Usages Act (maps available). Please observe the correct signalling, as follows:

- Interior lights on, headlights off: onlookers may watch but not participate.
- Interior lights on, headlights on: onlookers are welcome to join in – knock or hoot for admittance.
- Interior lights off, headlights on: onlookers are not welcome in any capacity.
- Interior lights off, headlights off: participants are here by mistake.

48

The War of the Worlds
by
H. G. WELLS

After a noisy afternoon trying to get on with the gardening as the Martians continued hammering on their machines and decimating bystanders, I decided to spruce myself up with a cold bath and an invigorating walk to the railway station, followed by tea. I must confess that the sight of all this Martian armament greatly excited me and after we'd finished the cheese course, I suggested to my wife that we might partake in a spot of sexual intercourse.

She agreed, also feeling somewhat energized by the potential obliteration of humanity. In fact, to my surprise, she insisted upon licking my whirlygigs, an act she hadn't offered since the late seventies, and, even more outlandishly, she then suggested I occupy her over the piano bench.

So immersed in our enjoyment were we, that at first we didn't notice the figure outside the window, it being slightly concealed by a mulberry bush. Indeed, my wife had now flipped over and was trying to lever herself over the top of the pianoforte, while I balanced on one knee, in an attempt to hoist myself up her windward passage. If I hadn't thought to close the curtains at that very moment I may never have seen it.

But there it was. Observing us, in flagrante, with its large dark-coloured eyes, which I noticed were placed rather oddly over a sensuous, if lipless, V-shaped mouth. Its oily, brown, gorgon tentacles quivered a little. I gasped. My wife, angling herself to see the source of my surprise, also started, but failed to scream, as I thought she must. The three of us stared at each other for a long hard minute; we all were aware of the awkwardness of this meeting, but none of us seemed able to break the intense eye contact.

And then our voyeur began to wave an octopus-like tentacle . . . and then another . . .

'By Jove, I think it wants to come in,' I murmured.

'Go, open the door and allow it passage within. I wish to lie with that Martian', replied my wife, her countenance solemn. I was surprised. I had not known my wife to be such a bobtail in all our marriage and so I obeyed.

A few moments later, we were gathered together; Man, Woman, Martian, devouring one another's bodies with feverish eyes. And then we moved, as one, and fell upon each other; a lustful hand upon a full breast, a curious tentacle caressing a penis, a lipless mouth biting a rosy buttock, which I thought might hurt but didn't. Our consummation was rapacious and peculiar. When we'd finished, we lay together until midnight, when the Martian suddenly oozed to its feet, donned my morning coat, I suppose as a disguise, and silently slid back out into the night, setting fire to the summerhouse as it left.

49

Sonnet 18
by
WILLIAM SHAKESPEARE

Shall I compare thee to a summer's day?
Thou art a hotter and more tempting mate.
My lips do suck your darling buds of May
And I did have my lease on our first date.
Sometimes too hot your eye of heaven shines
When round your golden hole my tongue has rimmed
And when with legs apart you do recline
Your nature is to leave yourself untrimmed;
But while the British summer stayest fair
Then we shall lose possession of our minds
And make love outside in the open air
Exposing to the sun our bare behinds.
So long as I can lie and you can wee
Be like our summer days and rain on me.

Fifty Shades of Grey
by
E. L. JAMES

Ana sat on the sofa in the Blue Room of Domesticity and adjusted her slippers. The end credits of *So You Think You Can Dance* were rolling on the television.

'Hurry up, Christian!' she called. 'It's nearly time for *Real Housewives of Beverly Hills*!'

Moments later, Christian came in, wearing his beige fleece dressing gown. There was a smear of dried egg down the front. She'd asked him to give it to her to put in the washing machine she didn't know how many times. He put the tray he was carrying down on the Ikea coffee table.

'Is that decaf?' she said, picking up her mug. 'You know it gives me gas.'

'If you wanted something else you should have said so,' said Christian. 'I asked you, like, five times.'

'I couldn't hear you, I had the TV on.'

'As per usual,' muttered Christian.

Ana took a sip of her drink anyway. If she was farting in bed tonight, it wasn't her problem.

'So . . . do you want to be tied up and beaten later?' asked Christian.

Ana bit her lip, but Christian had turned away and was busy sniffing the kitty litter, so he didn't seem to notice. She checked with her subconscious, but it was having a nap, and her Inner Goddess was doing some Hoovering.

'Do you mind if we skip it tonight?' she said. 'I'm premenstrual and really bloated. You know that's one of my hard limits.'

Christian didn't look that disappointed. 'How about a game of Scrabble instead?' he said.

'OK,' sighed Ana. She would have to let him win again. He was such a sore loser.

'So, you know the Red Room of Pain, well I was thinking that this weekend —' she began.

'You know I'm actually going to be pretty busy this weekend. I thought I should probably mow the lawn around the front moat,' Christian interjected, worried.

'Relax,' Ana reassured him, 'I just thought if you could shift your Nordic skis, which incidentally you haven't used since last Christmas, then we could convert it into something useful, like a craft room. I mean it's not like we ever use it any more.'

Christian shrugged. 'Whatever,' he said.

'We could redecorate it. There's a clearance sale at Macy's. I have a coupon.'

'Shush,' he admonished her. 'The show's starting.'

As Christian shovelled a handful of popcorn into his mouth, Ana felt herself missing her single days, and yearned for the comforts of a good book.

Acknowledgements

Thanks to Colin, Richard, Michael, Jose, Giorgio, Charlie, Annie, Peggy and Jim, Christylle and Nicholas, Robyn and the Ladies with Punch, and, of course, my excellent editor, Andreas.

Index

Pennines 116

Pesos, currency 88

Pequod, as gay party boat 95

Pickenfoot, Colonel 18

Piggy in the Middle, as coital arrangement 53

Popcote, Mr, shock of 19

Popcote, Mrs, shock of 19

Portrait, cancellation and possible incurring of a late fee of 33

Prostitutes 49, 69, 121

Pubic hair, lack of trimming of 131

Pyramids of Egypt 87

Raccoon up a chimney stack, as allegory for enthusiastic oral sex 33

Raspberry ripples 100

Reflective garments, safe masturbation within 126

Reins 24

Rennes, disappointing day trip to 18

Rhinoceros 99

Riding crop 66

Rimming 131

Rix, Graham, disappointing performance in penalty shoot-out of 12

Roibos tea 49

Rubber spatula 94

Rubber, stimulating odour of 69

Rue du Vieux Colombier, Paris 52

Rural milkman, as potential sexual partner 100

Russians, gigantic boobs of 72

Russians, resemblance of to Agent Provocateur models 72

Russians, speculation over what they ingest other than caviar and cock 72

Sadomasochism 2, 26, 27, 66, 70, 73, 122

Salad, Chicken Caesar 28

Samoyedic, Lithuania 103

Sand, as impediment for manual masturbation 89

Sand, as canvas for temporary erotic art 88

Sapphism 32

Sauna 24, 74

Schmetterling as epithet for vulva 85

Schnozzle 15

Seaman, David, inadvisability of lobbing from distance 12

Secret bud, as obnoxious euphemism for clitoris 19

Self-pleasuring, incessantness of, causing concern to parents 114

Sensor unit, placement in sparkplug socket 111

Sex with women, actually gayer than sex with men 29

Shadow puppets 76

Shandy, hand 20

Sheep 87

Shrimp cocktail, erotic potential of 4

Shrunken skull, as sexual aide 96

Sierra Leone 99

Signals, misreading of 38

Signals, for dogging 128

Size of cock, small, chances of entire office being told about 23

Skittles, superiority of purple and orange ones of 48

Skoda 92

Soccer Star sticker album, sexual desirability of completion of 10

Socks, kept on in hope of swift exit 125

Song, as displacement activity during bondage 27

Spa facilities, lack of 96

Spanish onions, likened to testicles 22

Splinters, hazards of 21

Stamboul–Calais coach, deviant sexual practices on 66

Stapleton, Frank, mercurial nature of 10

Starbuck, as maker of unappealing coffee 96

Starbuck, as unappealing potential sex partner 96

Subtitled films, duty watching of 48

Suede pumps, advisability of use of suede protection spray 101

Summer's day, comparison to 131

Swahili 97

Swinging 91